THE
COMPACT
D·I·S·C
BOOK

A Complete Guide to the

Digital Sound of the Future

BRYAN BREWER AND **EDD KEY**

HARCOURT BRACE JOVANOVICH, PUBLISHERS
San Diego New York London

Requests for permission to make copies of any
part of the work should be mailed to:
Permissions, Harcourt Brace Jovanovich, Publishers,
Orlando, Florida 32887.

Library of Congress Cataloging-in-Publication Data

Brewer, Bryan, 1946–
The compact disc book.

"A Harvest/HBJ book."
Bibliography: p.
1. Compact discs. 2. Compact disc players. I. Key,
Edd. II. Title.
TK7882.C56B74   1987   621.389′32   87-17706
ISBN 0-15-620050-3 (pbk.)

Designed by G.B.D. Smith

Printed in the United States of America

First edition

A B C D E

Contents

PART THREE
The Disc

PART FOUR
The CD in Perspective

Preface

When we first started writing about the Compact Disc in 1984, many people still had no idea what we were referring to. We even encountered stereo retail stores where salespeople needed coaching on the exciting capabilities of this brand-new technology. To most people the term CD still meant Certificate of Deposit.

But it hasn't taken long for music consumers to catch on. The CD's sound quality, convenience, and durability have pushed the Compact Disc revolution ahead with unprecedented speed. The players and discs are appearing on store shelves in rapidly increasing numbers. Magazines, radio, and television have helped spread the word about today's new digital sound.

This explosion of publicity about CD, in concentrating on the newest player models and the latest disc releases, has left an information gap about the Compact Disc: the story of what it is and how it works. This book is intended to fill that gap, giving you background and details on all aspects of the players and discs, including practical advice on how to make good purchases of each.

We have tried to give you enough of the technical background in simple terms so you can appreciate what you're hearing when you listen to a Compact Disc. It was never our intention to write a highly technical treatise on digital audio. Instead, we have attempted to interpret this new technology on a popular level. If you want more technical detail, you can consult the references given at the end of the book. Also, please note that we have mentioned specific products for illustrative purposes only; our mention of a product does not imply any endorsement on our part.

We would also like to give thanks to some of the people who have helped make this book a reality: to John Radziewicz, our editor at HBJ, for his friendly shepherding of the manuscript to its completion; to Paul Ackerman for his numerous drawings and photographs; to Dave Kaplan of Magnolia Hi-Fi and Bill Baker of Silver Platters for their help with arranging photo sessions; to all the helpful people who supplied photographs for use in the book; to Laura Buddine, Bert Gall, Theresa Holmes, Cheryl Lotz, Ken Pohlmann, and David Vernier for their helpful reviews of the manuscript; to Tom Tobin and Stephanie Weber for their understanding and support; to Molly Brewer for her patience with our working evenings and weekends; and to George Richards, Carl Compton, and all the other Earth Gospel Players for their special assistance with this project.

Finally, we would like to dedicate this book to the unsung heroes of the Compact Disc— the numerous executives and engineers from companies around the globe whose spirit of international cooperation has helped make the Compact Disc a worldwide standard.

BRYAN BREWER AND EDD KEY
SEATTLE, WASHINGTON

PART ONE

Introduction

CHAPTER I

The CD Revolution

"Of all the various forms of entertainment in the home, I know of nothing that compares with music. It is safe and sound, appeals to all the finer emotions, and tends to bind family influences with a wholesomeness that links old and young together."
— Thomas A. Edison

Since the Compact Disc and the Compact Disc player appeared in 1983, they have captured the imagination of the press and the record-buying public around the world. It would be no exaggeration to say that the enthusiasm which has greeted their appearance rivals the excitement aroused by Thomas Alva Edison's invention of the original phonograph over one hundred years ago.

But is the Compact Disc, or CD, truly the quantum leap in audio technology that the media and the advertisements have made it out to be? Or is it just another trendy electronic toy that will be replaced in a few years by the next "home entertainment miracle"? Let's take a look at some facts:

• By the end of 1986, three years after their introduction, CD players were selling at the rate of over a million per year. By contrast, it took the VCR three times as long to reach that mark, making the CD player the fastest-growing consumer electronic product ever introduced. Prices of players have plummeted from over $1000 initially to as little as $150.

• Every major record label is now actively releasing new albums and reissuing older music titles in CD format as fast as production will allow. Buyers can choose from over ten thousand disc titles representing every style of music —from classical to jazz, rock to country and western, experimental to comedy. Disc prices have dropped from an initial $20 each to the $10–$14 range.

• A highly successful new breed of "CD-only" record labels and retail stores is appearing throughout the country. Radio stations everywhere are boosting sales and listener awareness through CD broadcasts.

• A host of new uses for the Compact Disc are currently in development—uses that will ensure a rapid proliferation of further refinements and, in turn, new technical innovations.

So there is much more to the CD than industry hype. But these figures alone can't tell the story. The best way to understand the CD revolution is to experience the product—to look at it, touch it, play it, listen to it.

MEET THE CD

Compared to the LP record, the "Compact" Disc is indeed compact. It measures only 4¾ inches (120 mm) in diameter. You can easily hold it in the palm of your hand, and at a mere ½ ounce, it's feather-light. Underneath its smooth plastic surface, a thin layer of metallic film is etched with billions of microscopic indentations, called *pits*, that form a three-mile-long spiral track on the disc.

Unlike a conventional turntable, which drags a needle through the groove on a record, a CD player aims a narrow beam of light from a low-powered laser at the track of pits. As the disc spins inside the player, the beam passes through the clear plastic, strikes the pits, and is reflected off the metallic film. This creates a flickering light whose pulses correspond to the sequence of the pits. This sequence is a

series of numerical, or *digital*, codes which represent the audio recorded on the disc. Electronic circuits in the player translate the sequence of pulses into the sound you hear.

The key word here is digital. With the Compact Disc, consumer audio has entered the computer age. The *digital audio* technology of the CD reproduces recorded sound with a degree of quality higher than previously possible.

Despite its sophisticated laser and computer technology, the CD player is designed to fit right in with your current audio components. Its styling is similar to cassette decks and VCRs. And the CD player works with any stereo system that has common auxiliary or tape input jacks. You don't need a new amplifier or speakers.

CD players are also remarkably easy to use. Simply turn the power on and press

the OPEN button. The player smoothly extends the disc tray for you to drop in your favorite CD. Press PLAY and the music begins.

The Convenient CD

The Compact Disc adds a dimension of convenience not possible with LP records and cassette tapes. It offers the most improvements over the LP, which it is primarily intended to replace. To begin with, you don't need to adjust or replace anything on a

The SONY CDP-620ES CD player and Don Dorsey's chart-topping *BACH-BUSTERS* disc of synthesized baroque music.

CD player. Its laser will function for thousands of hours of playback. It is much easier to use than the turntable's sensitive tone arm and doesn't need frequent replacement like a stylus cartridge. Moreover, the CD player is far less sensitive to movement during play than the phonograph. No more tiptoeing past the stereo system when your favorite song is playing.

A unique, unprecedented benefit of the CD is instant access to any track on the disc. Borrowing from computer technology, the CD's digital data storage system assigns each grouping of audio data on the disc its own unique "address." If you want to hear track 10, the push of a button will send the laser directly to that track—often in less than a second. And to keep you up to date, the number 10 appears on a luminescent display on the front of the player. Along with the current track number, you'll also find on the display useful information such as the playing time of the track or the disc.

The CD's push-button access to music means you no longer have to position the tone arm carefully over the LP's lead-in groove, or fast-forward or reverse the cassette to get the song you want. Push a button and your choice is instantly played.

The Durable CD

Unlike your LP or tape collection, your CDs, with a little care, will hardly show the passage of time—regardless of how often the discs are played. In fact, they could easily outlive your grandchildren. The reason for this incredible durability can be found just a millimeter under the disc's plastic surface.

Hold the CD's underside up to the light and you'll see a dazzling spectrum of color given off by the silvery heart of the disc. Invisible to the naked eye, the spiral of pits consists of almost two billion indentations in the plastic of the disc. They convey the digital information the player uses to recreate the recorded sound.

Because the player "reads" the information from the disc with a light, nothing ever touches its surface. That means no wear and tear on the CD. Except for scratches caused by rough handling, it is theoretically immortal.

The Programmable CD

As with an LP or tape, you can let a CD play along from first song to last. But a major advancement in music playback comes from the CD's programmability. It allows you to designate the order in which you hear the selections of music on the disc.

A memory chip in the circuitry of most players can store a series of selections—usually about 15—which you program for playback in the desired order, excluding tracks you don't want to hear. And most players also

improvement over older stereo components—especially turntables—among which there is a vast range of quality.

It is the CD's superb sound quality that first caught the ear of record buyers, and it is the same quality that pulls in new converts at a rate of some 10,000 new CD-player owners per day in the U.S. alone.

PLAYERS AND DISCS FOR EVERYONE

Today's CD players can accompany you from the living room, to the car, to work, to the beach. Regardless of your lifestyle, listening habits, or budget, the variety of players gives you ample op-

The versatile CD player can be used at home, as a portable, or in the car. Home players connect to a stereo system; portables are battery-operated; and auto players are installed in a car stereo system.

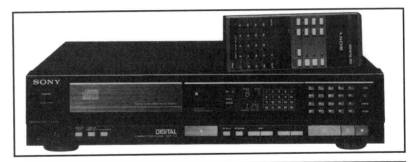

portunity to become a CD convert.

The range of choices for home CD players is expanding as more features are added every year. For example, some players now "remember" your favorite sequence of tracks for a disc, even after you turn off power to the player. Other players now reaching the market at affordable prices can hold between 5 and 10 discs at a time.

Portable CD players are getting smaller and lighter and capable of longer battery playback time. 1987 saw the introduction of several portables measuring less than one-inch thick. And "boom box" models, with self-contained CD, cassette, radio, and speakers, continue to sell well.

CD players for the car are rapidly advancing in shock resistance and miniaturization. They come in CD/radio combination styles that easily fit in a car dashboard. One model stores 10 discs in a trunk unit; only the controls are mounted on the dash.

The selection of available discs spans every style and era of recorded music, from Bach to Basie to the Beach Boys; from vintage recordings to the latest releases; from movie soundtracks to original cast performances; from foreign-language training to aerobic workouts.

Also, the price of CDs is coming down. Many CD pressing plants have been operating around the clock to satisfy eager new music consumers. As disc manufacturing capacity begins to catch up with the demand, the cost of the average disc is sure to drop to the $10 level soon.

The hi-fi and record industries have made it easy—almost irresistible—for you to upgrade to a CD. The push-button convenience of the player, the compactness and durability of the disc, and the startling clarity of the sound speak for themselves. The digital sound of the future has arrived.

Over ten thousand CD titles are available in virtually all styles of music.

20 QUESTIONS ABOUT THE COMPACT DISC

1. What's the Best CD-Player Brand to Buy?

There is no right answer to this question, any more than someone can tell you what is the best car to buy. There are almost two hundred CD-player models on the market, and most of them offer good value in terms of features and quality. You'll find helpful guidelines in Chapter 5 for selecting a CD player.

2. What Are the Main Differences between CD Players?

Surprisingly enough, sound quality is fairly uniform among CD players. Yes, there are a few dogs and a few super systems, but the great majority of CD players sound quite similar to the average listener. The major differences are in the features offered, such as programmability, remote control, and multi-disc capability, as well as the quality of the electronic components.

3. What Features Should I Look for in a CD Player?

It all depends on your listening habits, your lifestyle, and your budget. The extensive list of features in Chapter 4 can help you narrow your choice.

4. Is the Laser in a CD Player Dangerous?

No. First of all, it only emits light when there's a disc in the player. Second, the power of the laser is very weak. And third, the beam is tightly focused very close to the disc, so that even if it could pass beyond the disc, its energy would be scattered very quickly.

5. Is CD Compatible with My Current Stereo System?

By all means. CD players have standard stereo plugs for connection to your amplifier or headphones. Although the increased sound capacity of CD may spur you to upgrade other components of your stereo system, an upgrade is certainly not necessary. See Chapter 5 for tips on upgrading your stereo system for CD.

6. What Makes Digital Audio Sound So Good?

The digital precision of the CD's computer technology gives a more accurate representation of audio than does an LP or a cassette. The result is a wider range of soft and ▶

loud sounds, and a truer reproduction of the entire spectrum of sounds audible to the human ear. Also, the increased clarity of digital recordings is due to the lack of tape hiss and the absence of fluctuations in playback speed.

7. Are All CD Recordings Created Equal?

No. Although the CD stores sound digitally, not all available discs contain music that was *recorded* digitally. Discs with digitally recorded music usually have quieter and cleaner sound, but that doesn't necessarily make them better. After all, it's the musical performance that makes the difference. The best guide is to listen to the disc before buying it or to refer to the opinions of your friends or disc reviewers. Chapter 7

covers digital audio recording.

8. What Kind of Music Sounds Best on CD?

The music you like to listen to. That's not a facetious answer, since almost all kinds of music can now be found on Compact Disc. And they all benefit from the CD's high sound quality.

9. Will CDs Totally Replace LPs?

Probably. How many record companies still make 78-rpm records?

10. Can You Get Sound on Both Sides of a CD?

While it is theoretically possible to have double-sided CDs, it doesn't make economic sense. It's cheaper to manufacture two single-sided discs, each of which can hold up

to 74 minutes of stereo sound. Furthermore, a disc with data stored on both sides would have no place for the label describing its contents.

11. Why Are CDs So Expensive?

CDs are made in a high-tech manufacturing environment that involves a *clean room* that must be kept virtually dust-free. Other complex processes add to the basic manufacturing cost, which in 1987 was about $2 per disc. That works out to about $15 retail when you add packaging, royalties, record label profit, and merchandiser's markup. See Chapter 6 to find out more about how CDs are made.

12. Will the Price of CDs Come Down?

Yes. When supply catches up with demand— probably in 1988—you will almost certainly begin to see lower prices. Also, new mastering and manufacturing processes may further help drive down the price of CDs.

13. Do CDs Wear Out?

No, at least not from normal handling and playback. The audio information is imbedded in the plastic structure of the disc. Nothing but laser light touches it. With normal care, a CD will sound as good in 50 years as it does today.

14. Is It OK If a CD Gets Scratched?

Some scratches on a CD will not affect the sound quality, certainly not to the extent that slight scratches on a record will cause a skip. This is because all CD players have built-in error-correction capability that can make

up for audio data that are obscured by small scratches. Large scratches can cause a disc to play improperly.

15. Do I Need a Disc Cleaner for My CD Collection?

A properly operating CD cleaner will certainly not hurt your discs. However, if you handle them carefully, you won't need a special cleaner. See Chapter 8 for more information on CD accessories.

16. What Maintenance Is Necessary for a CD Player?

None. There is nothing to clean or adjust or replace.

17. Will a CD Player Wear Out?

Like any mass-produced electronics item, a CD player will not last forever. Eventually the laser

or the motors may need replacement. But statistics so far indicate that most CD players will play for many years of normal consumer use.

18. Where's the Best Place to Buy a CD Player?

If you're interested primarily in price, a discount store or mail-order operation might be best for you. But if you want intelligent help in making the best selection as well as service after the sale, you may be better off at a reputable stereo store. See Chapter 5 for guidelines on buying a CD player.

19. Can I Record on CD?

Not with today's technology. The pits on a Compact Disc are permanently molded in the plastic at the manufacturing plant. Although expensive in- ▶

dustrial equipment exists for laser recording of data, the cost and practicality of a consumer-recordable CD is uncertain.

20. Can a CD Store More Than Sound?

A Compact Disc can store any digital data, not just digital audio. CD–ROM (Read-Only-Memory) systems have been in use since 1985 to store massive text data bases for use with a computer. And the forthcoming CD-Interactive systems for home entertainment and education will store sound, TV pictures, text, and programs all on the same disc. Chapters 9 and 10 describe these exciting uses.

CHAPTER 2

Fundamentals of Digital Audio

The Compact Disc logo includes the words "Digital Audio." It's a reminder that the audio on a CD is encoded in digital form, much like computer data. Most of the CD's benefits are a direct result of storing sound this way. Digital audio provides clearer, cleaner, and crisper sound than records or tapes. And the CD's instant access and programming capabilities

are possible because of the digital encoding of specific addresses for every location on the disc.

For most of its history, recorded sound has been stored not as digital data but as *analog* information. Analog audio simply means that the recording medium stores a physical representation (literally an analog) of the shape of the original sound wave. Edison's original phonograph, 78-rpm records, vinyl LPs, cassette and reel-to-reel tapes—all store sound as analog audio.

You can enjoy the CD's sound quality and conve-

nience without knowing anything about the principles of digital audio. Drop the disc into the player and push the PLAY button. This simplicity has contributed much to the success of the Compact Disc. You get all the high-quality benefits without high-tech hassle.

However, if you want to go beyond the basics of push-button music, you may need a little background information. For example, if you want to be able to talk to a stereo salesperson about players that use "oversampling," you first need to know what *sampling* is. If you want to evaluate a disc that was recorded in analog and mastered in digital, it will help to know the difference between analog and digital audio. If you read about a player with "dual DACs," you might first want to know what a single DAC (or *digital-to-analog converter*) does.

This chapter presents the fundamentals of digital audio, explaining and illustrating the technical terms. The mathematics of the explanations do not go beyond basic arithmetic, nor does this chapter assume that you have any prior technical knowledge of recording or electronics. What's presented here is a foundation for making intelligent decisions about your investment in digital audio.

ANALOG AND DIGITAL

Sound is created when energy is released as vibrations in a physical medium such as air. For example, drawing a bow across a violin string causes the string to vibrate and disturb the surrounding air. Sound waves travel outward from the string to be reflected, absorbed, or dissipated. When the sound waves reach your eardrum, you hear the sound of the violin.

The rate of vibration, or *frequency*, determines the pitch of the sound. The faster the vibration, the higher the pitch. Sound or *acoustical* frequencies are expressed in *hertz* (abbreviated Hz), which stands for the number of vibrations, or cycles, per second. For example, musicians often tune instruments to *concert A* pitch, a tone with a frequency of 440 Hz. A violin string tuned to this pitch moves back and forth 440 times each second. Frequencies above 1000 Hz are often expressed in *kilohertz* (kHz), or thousands of cycles per second.

The range of human hearing extends from about 20 Hz (a low, barely audible hum, like a diesel engine in the distance) to about 20 kHz (a high-pitched hiss, like compressed air escaping). Some adults have lost the ability to hear much above the 15-kHz level, and additional hearing loss generally occurs with age. But since much of the sound energy of speech and music is below 10 or 12 kHz, the loss of high-frequency hearing does not affect the ability to understand speech or to hear music. For those who can hear that high the upper frequencies add subtle tone and coloration to music and voices.

Sound waves of all audible frequencies can be recorded. When the sound of a singer's voice, for instance, reaches a microphone, the sound vibrates a mechanism inside which creates an electrical signal. The frequency of that electrical signal corresponds to the acoustical frequency, or pitch, of the singer's voice. This electrical signal can be displayed as an audio *waveform*, which is essentially a picture of the sound wave vibrations of the voice as they change over time.

An audio waveform varies in shape according to the sound it represents. A pure tone, such as that produced by a flute, creates a simple, smooth-shaped waveform. Complex sounds, such as voices and combinations of instruments, create wave-forms with many irregularities.

Whereas the frequency of a waveform determines the pitch, it is the height, or *amplitude*, of the waveform that determines the loudness. The greater the amplitude, the louder the sound. The same holds true for the violin string: the farther it vibrates back and forth, the louder it sounds.

The voltage of the electrical signal produced by the microphone is continually changing to reflect the changes in the loudness of the audio being picked up by the microphone. When repre-sented graphically, these changes appear as variations in the amplitude of the wave-form. For example, the electrical signal of a 440-Hz tone changes amplitude, fluctuating up and down to create the waveform, 440 times every second. This corresponds to the violin string moving back and forth 440 times every second.

Thus, the electrical signal from the microphone carries frequencies that correspond to the acoustical frequencies of the sound, as well as changing voltages that correspond to the changes in the volume of the sound. The goal of any audio recording system, therefore, is to capture these two characteristics: the amplitude and frequency information of the audio waveform.

A recording system typically includes a microphone, a recording machine, a storage medium, a playback machine, and an amplifier/speaker combination.

The recording machine

A pure tone consists of a single frequency and creates a simple, smooth-shaped waveform. Most sound we hear is in the form of complex waveforms, which contain many frequencies.

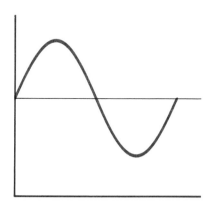

Pure-tone Waveform

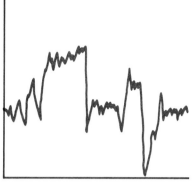

Complex Waveform

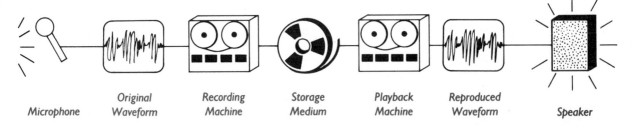

| Microphone | Original Waveform | Recording Machine | Storage Medium | Playback Machine | Reproduced Waveform | Speaker |

All sound recording systems use a recording machine, a storage medium, and a playback machine to reproduce the recorded audio waveforms.

uses the electrical signal from the microphone to create a representation of the changing waveform and store it on some type of medium. Later, a compatible playback device uses the recorded information to recreate a close approximation of the original waveform. This recreated analog signal is amplified and sent to the speaker to reproduce the sound as vibrations in air. The higher the quality of the recording and playback systems, the more the reproduced sound resembles the original sound.

The storage medium for the sound can be either ana-log or digital. In the case of analog, the audio is stored as a physical representation of the original waveform. For example, the tiny squiggles in the groove of an LP, when viewed under a microscope, resemble the shape of the recorded waveform. The squiggles are the "analog" of the original sound. When the needle moves along the groove, the squiggles cause the needle to vibrate, just as the mechanism in the microphone vibrated when the recording was made. The needle's vibrations are turned into an electrical signal, which is then amplified and played back through a speaker.

A cassette tape also contains an analog of the waveform, stored as fluctuations in the magnetic field of the particles on the tape. The magnetic head on a tape player senses these fluctuations and creates an electrical signal for playback through an amplifier/speaker system.

A digital recording, however, does not contain an analog image of the waveform. There is no direct physical representation of the waveform's shape. A digital audio recording system contains electronic circuits that convert the electrical signal from the microphone into a series of numerical, or *digital*, data. The pits on a Compact Disc represent numbers that mathematically define the shape of the waveform.

When the CD player rotates the disc so that the track of pits moves past the laser beam, the player measures the reflected light to determine the length and sequence of the pits. Electronic circuits in the player translate the pit measurements into a stream of digital data. Other circuits use the numerical information in the digital data to convert the recorded waveforms back into an analog electrical signal. This in turn is fed through the audio output connectors on the player. The signal is amplified by the stereo system and played back through speakers or headphones.

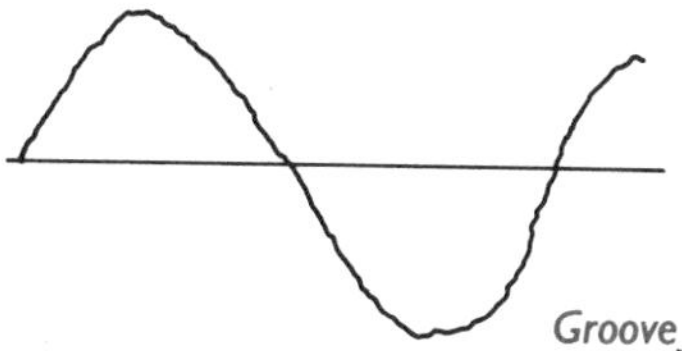

Analog Waveform

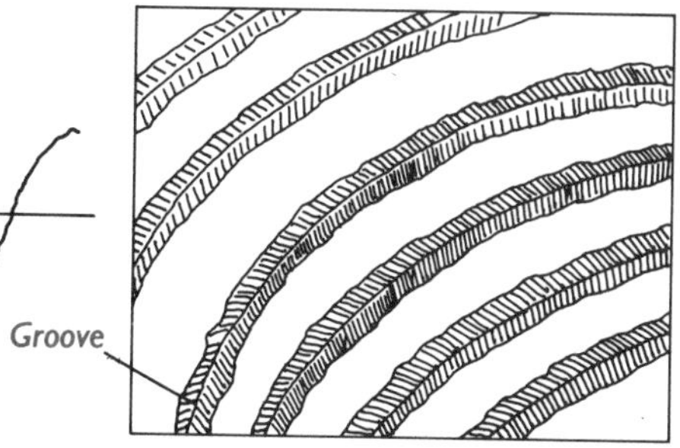

Groove

LP Record (close-up)

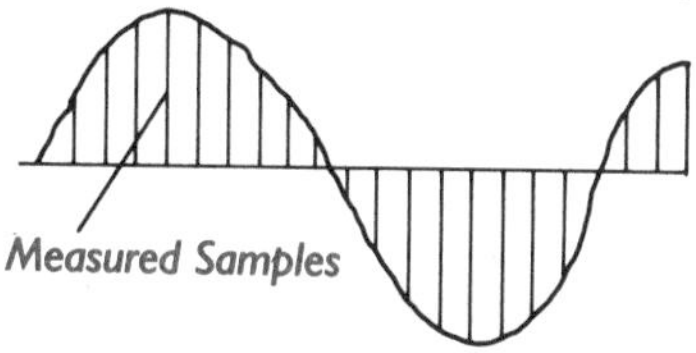

Measured Samples

Digitized Waveform

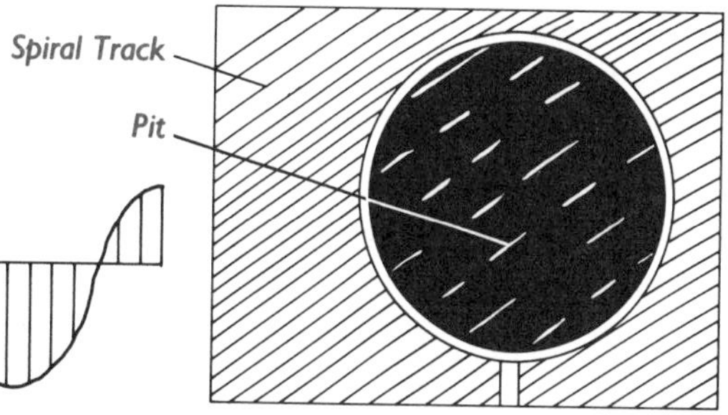

Spiral Track

Pit

Compact Disc (close-up)

SAMPLING AND QUANTIZATION

Both analog and digital recordings store information about the frequency and the amplitude of the sound waveform. In an analog system, the audio remains in analog form

An analog waveform follows the contour of the original sound waves. A digital waveform divides each sound wave into measured sections (samples) and records each as a numerical value.

throughout, from microphone to storage medium to playback through a speaker. In a digital recording system, the analog waveform must be converted

An LP record stores sound as squiggles in a groove—actual physical representations of the shape of the original sound waveforms. A Compact Disc stores sound as pits in a track—numerical representations of the digitized waveforms.

to digital data before it can be stored.

At the heart of every digital recording system is an electronic circuit called an *analog-to-digital converter*, or ADC. The ADC circuit analyzes the shape of the sound waveform and represents it with numerical codes. It does this by measuring the varying voltage of the electrical signal from the microphone and converting those measurements into digital data. This measurement process does not happen continuously, but occurs at discrete points in time. The ADC takes readings of the electrical signal at regular intervals and computes their digital value. Each of these values is called a *sample*. The numerical values of these samples are represented by the pits on the CD. This measurement and conversion process is known as *digitizing* or *sampling* the sound. The rate at which an ADC samples sound—its *sampling rate*—is also expressed in Hz or kHz. The sampling rate for CD audio is 44.1 kHz. This means the ADC takes a sample of the audio for each stereo channel (left and right)

every $1/44,100$th of a second, or every 22.6 microseconds.

Basic digital audio theory requires that the sampling rate of a digital recording system be at least twice as high as the highest frequency sound it can store. This permits the samples to represent both a *peak* and *valley* value of the amplitude of the highest frequency sound. Thus the main reason for setting the CD sampling rate in the 40-kHz range is to allow the CD to store sounds up to the 20-kHz limit of human hearing. The 10 percent above 40 kHz allows some extra leeway in the recording process. The precise rate of 44,100 was chosen because this number can be evenly divided in numerous ways, a fact which contributes to the efficient storage and manipulation of the samples as numerical data.

When you play a CD, a device in the player called a *digital-to-analog converter* (DAC) converts the digital samples recorded on the disc

back into an analog electrical signal representing the original waveform. This signal is reconstructed at the same rate as the sampling rate to maintain the frequency information of the recorded waveform.

Represented graphically, the horizontal scale indicates time, with each interval representing successive samples. CD audio has 44,100 samples per second. The vertical scale indicates the value of each sample, i.e., the height, or amplitude, of the waveform at any point. For CD audio, the value of each sample is measured on this scale in equal increments from 0 to 65,535. This process of subdividing the amplitude into increments is called *quantization*.

The 65,535 increments result from CD audio's use of 16 *bits* to store information about each sample. (For an explanation of bits, see the box on the binary number system.) The analog-to-digital converter measures the

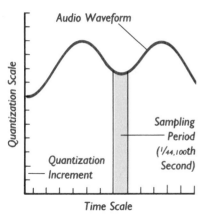

Audio Waveform

Quantization Scale

Sampling Period (¹/₄₄,₁₀₀th Second)

Quantization Increment

Time Scale

A digital audio recorder measures, or samples, the waveform at regular intervals in time (44,100 times per second for the CD). The value of each sample is measured in quantization increments (from 0 to 65,535 for the CD). The sampling periods preserve the frequency of the waveform, or pitch of the sound. The quantization measurements preserve the amplitude of the waveform, or loudness of the sound.

amplitude of each sample and assigns it a value in the range from 0 to 65,535. The value is stored not as a decimal number, however, but as a 16-bit binary number comprised of zeroes and ones.

The CD's 16-bit quantiza-tion provides a choice of 65,535 different incremental values that can be assigned to any sample. This substantial spread provides two major audible benefits.

First, there is far less inherent system noise. Compared to analog systems, CD digital audio approximates the actual value of the amplitude of the original waveform in greater detail, resulting in more precise sound. The second benefit of 16-bit quantization is an increase in the range—compared to the LP or cassette—between the loudest and the softest sound the disc can store. The large number of incremental values allows the CD to reproduce a very wide range of volume levels. Both factors contrib-

THE BINARY NUMBER SYSTEM

Unlike our ordinary decimal number system (which uses 10 digits, 0 through 9), the binary number system uses only two digits: zero and one. A bit—short for *binary digit*—has either the value 0 or the value 1. Computers use the binary number system to store data as bits because simple electronic circuits can represent a 1 or a 0 by the presence or the absence of electrical voltage. If the circuit has voltage, the bit is a 1; if not, it's a 0. In other words, "on" corresponds to a 1, and "off" corresponds to a 0. Representing data as "digits" like this is the root of the term "digital."

As with the decimal number system, the binary digits 0 and 1 are combined to represent larger values. It's easiest to visualize this process by comparing binary values with their *decimal equivalent* (the decimal number equal in value to the binary number). The simple values 0 and 1 are identical in each system. To represent the next higher value in decimal, we ▶

ute to the virtual absence of noise during silent intervals on a CD recording.

There's little doubt that the sound of CD digital audio is an improvement over LPs and cassette tapes. Both these analog systems are limited by the inherent physical properties of their storage media. They depend on squiggles in a groove or magnetic fluctuations on a tape to represent highly complex information. Both media introduce significant noise and cannot provide sufficient detail to accurately reproduce high frequencies.

Because CD audio stores such a finely measured representation of sound as a series of numbers, it does not suffer from the system noise and frequency limitations of consumer analog audio. In fact, when the CD digital audio signal is set to all zeroes, it adds no noise whatsoever to the sound reproduction system. A zero digital state means absolute silence. Digital *does* make a difference.

use the decimal digit 2. But the binary system has no more single digits, so it moves to its next highest value: 10. This binary 10 has the decimal equivalent of 2. The next value, binary 11, equals decimal 3; binary 100 equals decimal 4; and so on:

Binary number	Decimal equivalent
0	0
1	1
10	2
11	3
100	4
101	5
110	6
111	7
1000	8
1001	9
1010	10
1011	11
1100	12
1101	13
1110	14
1111	15
10000	16
10001	17
....	....
....	....
1111111111111011	65,531
1111111111111100	65,532
1111111111111101	65,533
1111111111111110	65,534
1111111111111111	65,535

▶

Just as the binary digits are combined in this way, combinations of computer circuits can represent larger binary values. It would take one circuit, representing one bit, to store the value 0 or 1. Two circuits could store two bits, or values through binary 11 (decimal 3). It takes three bits to store values through decimal 7; four bits for values through 15; and so on. Of interest here is the capacity of a 16-bit binary number: it can store values from 0 to decimal 65,535. All 16 bits, including leading zeroes, are stored for each value. Thus the 16-bit number representing the decimal value 14 is 0000000000001110.

CD ENCODING AND PLAYBACK

Before audio can be stored on a CD, it must be recorded. The original recording is typically made on a tape recording system, which may be either analog or digital. (See Chapter 7 for more details on recording for a CD.)

The original recording must then be encoded in a format suitable for storage on the CD. These steps take place at a mastering studio and at the disc manufacturing plant, using equipment especially designed for CD encoding.

The encoding process—sampling a sound and storing it as digital audio data—is called *pulse code modulation*, or PCM. The *pulses* in PCM are the samples, the measurements of a waveform's amplitude in short time intervals. The *code* represents the numerical values of the measurements. *Modulation* is simply a means of encoding information for storage or transmission.

You may be familiar with other modulation techniques such as amplitude modulation (AM) and frequency modulation (FM), which have long been used for the transmission of radio frequencies. For storing digital audio, PCM is the preferred method.

Encoding

The basic PCM encoding process for CD stereo (left and right channels) includes several major steps shown below. If the original recording is digital, some of the initial steps will have already taken place in the recording process.

The first major step is *input filtering* of the analog electrical signal. An audio filter is an electronic circuit that permits only certain frequencies of sound to pass through, filtering out unwanted frequencies. In this case, the input filters suppress all frequencies above the 20-kHz range.

If higher frequencies were allowed to pass through to the sampling stage, they would interact with lower frequencies to create false au-

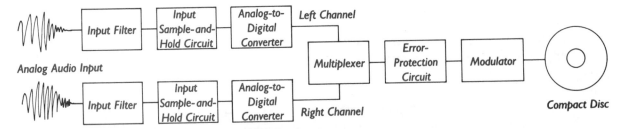

PCM encoding for the CD transforms an analog waveform into the proper sequence of digital data for storage on the disc.

dio tones called *alias* signals. If these alias signals were sampled and stored on the CD, you would hear them as extraneous noise during the playback of the recording. That's why well-designed digital audio recording systems have efficient input filters, sometimes called *anti-aliasing* filters to screen out these unwanted frequencies from the input signal.

After input filtering, the electrical signal—still in analog form—goes to a *sample-and-hold* circuit, which samples the waveform precisely every ¼₄, ₁₀₀th of a second. It holds the analog value of a sample long enough for the analog-to-digital converter to compute the 16-bit binary number closest to the measured amplitude of the sample. After the ADC determines the numerical value of the sample, it creates the corresponding bit pattern—now in the digital realm—and sends it to the next stage.

Once the left and right channels have been sampled and converted into digital values, they are ready to be combined into a single data stream. This is accomplished by the *multiplexer*, a circuit that combines the output bit patterns for each channel into a serial stream of bits that is then fed to the *error-protection* stage.

The ability to protect against errors in the audio data is one of the biggest advantages of the Compact Disc. Data errors can occur in the manufacturing process or result from scratches on the disc. Since digital audio is composed of bits that can be counted exactly, the encoding system calculates precise formulas that are used to spot data errors during playback. The results of these formulas, called *check codes* and *parity bits*, are added to the data stream at this point in the encoding process. These error-correction codes, by defining the numerical interrelationships of groups of data on the disc, provide a dependable blueprint for reconstructing any missing or erroneous data.

An additional part of the error-protection scheme is

called *interleaving*. Electronic circuits subdivide the multiplexed data stream into segments, each of which contains some of the error-correction codes for adjacent segments. The data stream is then reordered so that segments originally adjacent to each other will be spread out, or interleaved, on the disc.

Should a defect on the disc obscure several adjacent segments, the data stored there are not necessarily lost. During playback, the player restores the data stream to its original order so that segments with missing data are rejoined with segments that were originally adjacent and which contain the error-correction codes necessary to reconstruct the sound.

The final step of preparing digital audio for storage on CD uses another modulation technique called *eight-to-fourteen modulation*, or EFM. (See Chapter 6 for details on EFM.) EFM encodes the zeroes and ones of the binary bit stream into a signal that can be better represented by the pits on the disc. Electronic circuits perform the modulation, which increases the efficiency of the data storage.

Synchronization codes, which help maintain proper disc speed during playback, are added at this stage as well. Following modulation, the data are ready for storage on a CD.

Playback

When you play back the disc in your CD player, the data from the disc go through playback steps that correspond in reverse order to the recording steps.

This time the process occurs in your player. First the laser light reflected from the pits is *demodulated* back into the encoded audio data. Next, the data are *de-interleaved* and analyzed for errors. If any errors are detected, circuits in the player use the

Decoding digital audio from a CD reverses the steps of the encoding process. (This diagram shows a decoding system with dual digital-to-analog converters and analog output filtering that occurs after the data are converted into analog form.)

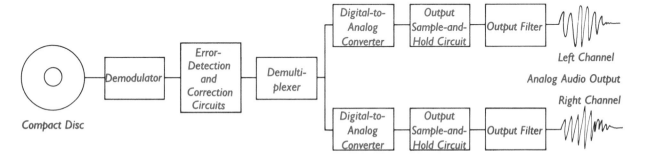

error-correction codes to re-construct the missing data.

Then the digital data are *demultiplexed* back into their left and right channels and fed to the digital-to-analog converters where the bit values of the samples are converted back to analog values. (In players with a single digital-to-analog converter, the signal is demultiplexed *after* conversion into analog.) An output sample-and-hold circuit reconstructs the sample values into an analog audio signal which is then filtered to smooth it out. Finally, the signal is sent to your stereo system and played back through speakers.

The trip that sound makes from the microphone in the recording studio to the pits on the disc and back out through your speakers is an incredibly complex one. It involves highly sophisticated equipment and the accurate processing of billions of bits of data for each disc—all happening at the remarkable rate of 44,100 times per sec-ond for each stereo channel. Yet the true marvel of CD digital audio is perhaps not so much its superb sound quality or powerful process-ing capabilities, but the successful packaging of this complex technology in a simple-to-use consumer product.

HOW LASERS AND COMPUTERS MAKE CD DIGITAL AUDIO POSSIBLE

The basic theory of digital audio was developed some fifty years prior to the advent of the CD. But for most of that time, the technology was not available to implement the concepts. It was not until the 1970s that the optical disc and the microprocessor reached levels of development so that the two could be merged in a single digital audio system.

Storing sound digitally requires an immense amount of data. For example, one second of sound from the CD uses over one million bits of data. You need a very dense digital storage medium to accommodate any significant amount of digital audio. If you stored CD audio on a magnetic floppy disc from an IBM Personal Computer, a single disc would hold less than three seconds of sound, hardly adequate for home entertainment.

The solution to the storage problem arrived in the form of the laser-encoded and laser-read optical disc. Because a laser beam can be focused to such a small point of light (about $\frac{1}{25,000}$th of an inch, or 1 micrometer wide), it can read information that is tightly packed together. A CD stores the data for one second of audio on an accumulated total area smaller than a pinhead. This means 15 billion bits—enough for 74 minutes of stereo sound—can be stored on a single disc.

The other challenge of digital audio is to process all those bits fast enough to keep up with the continuous playback of music. Again, the 1970s produced the answer: microchips. Rapid advances in microprocessor technology enabled engineers to cram more and more processing power onto single chips. The decrease in size—and price—of the electronic components required for digital audio systems has made the CD possible.

In reality, a Compact Disc player is a very powerful computer. But it is much different from a personal computer which you can program for a variety of tasks. A CD player is designed only for the functions involved in decoding the data from the disc and turning them back into sound; programming a CD player today is limited to entering track sequences. The common heritage of CD players and computers is reflected in the audio industry's use of the computer terms *hardware* and *software* to refer to the players and the discs.

PART TWO

The
Player

CHAPTER 3

On the Beam:
How the Player Works

From the outside, a Compact Disc player doesn't appear very different from any other piece of stereo equipment. The buttons, numeric displays, and standard connecting cords, along with the contemporary styling of the units, let the CD merge unobtrusively with your home entertainment center. The portable Sony "Discman" can easily be mistaken for a large Sony "Walkman" cassette player. And automobile CD models are specifically designed to fit into standard dashboard slots.

A glance inside the player also shows similarities to other audio and video equipment. The maze of chips and electronic components, soldered to printed-circuit boards and connected with various colored wires, may look much like any other electronic gear.

But the similarities are deceptive. A CD player functions in a radically different manner. Its computer and laser technologies work together to perform the most sophisticated processing done in any consumer electronics product.

The computer technology is represented by the storage of audio as numerical codes and the microchips used to interpret those codes. This results in the high degree of accuracy, integrity, and accessibility of disc data.

The laser technology is represented by the optical disc itself and the laser which reads it. Because of the microscopic focus of the laser, an optical disc can contain massive amounts of data in a very small area. The 14-square-inch data area of a CD holds over fifteen billion bits of data for its 74 minutes of stereo sound.

CD-PLAYER SYSTEMS

The task of a CD player is to read those bits from the disc and recreate the sound encoded there. To do this, a player has five basic systems, each of which closely coordinates its activities with the functioning of the other systems. The five systems within a player are:

1. The Disc Drive System: a spindle to hold the disc and a motor to rotate the disc at varying speeds.
2. The Laser Pickup System: a laser, a light-sensitive detector cell, and a set of lenses and mirrors to direct the laser's light beam.
3. The Servo System: several small *servomechanisms* that make extremely precise adjustments to the position of the laser pickup to maintain proper motor speed, focus, and tracking of the disc.
4. The Data Decoding System: a series of electronic circuits that translate the raw data from the disc into the audio output signal.
5. The Control and Display System: the central microprocessor of the CD player that coordinates its entire operation.

The Disc Drive System

The CD player's disc drive system is located inside the unit, behind the drawer or door in which you insert the

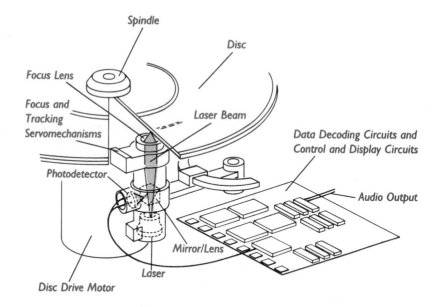

A CD player includes internal systems to spin the disc at the proper speed, maintain focus and tracking of the laser beam, decode the data into audio output, and manage the controls and display panel of the player.

disc. Once inside the player, the disc is mounted on a spindle so that it can be rotated for the laser pickup to scan. To ensure a firm positioning of the disc and to compensate for any warpage and inconsistent symmetry, most players clamp the disc into place with a clamping device at the center.

The operation of a CD disc drive is far more complex than the phonograph turntable, which consists of a simple motor that spins the LP at the constant speeds of 33⅓, 45, or 78 rpm. By contrast, the CD disc-drive motor spins the CD at a continually varying speed, ranging from 500 rpm to 200 rpm. This keeps the spiral track of pits moving past the laser pickup at a constant rate. When the beam is reading the inner portion of the disc, the faster revolutions keep the linear scanning rate between 1.2 and 1.4 meters per second. Near the outer edge, the disc spins more slowly to maintain the same linear velocity. Variable speed rotation ensures a constant flow of data to the processing circuitry from every point on the disc.

Synchronization pulses embedded in the data flow supply the timing informa-tion used to keep the disc spinning at the proper speed. The *CD controller*, a micro-processor in the control and display system, compares these pulses with an internal quartz-crystal clock and cal-culates the necessary adjust-ments to the speed. The con-troller signals a mechanism called the *motor drive servo*, which in turn regulates the speed of the motor.

The Laser Pickup System

The "eye" of the CD player is located in the laser pickup, most of which mea-sure no more than one inch in any dimension. The pickup aims the laser beam from below the disc to read the information encoded on the data surface of its under-side. The pickup begins play-back at the inner edge of the disc and moves along the spi-ral track toward the outer edge as the disc plays.

Depending on your player, the laser pickup assembly slides along a small set of tracks or swings on a pivot like a turntable tone arm, covering a distance of about an inch and a half between the inner and outer edges of the recording area of the disc. When playing, the laser pickup slowly follows the spiral track outward, but when responding to push-button commands, it moves quickly to a selected point on the disc.

The laser pickup contains three parts which work to-gether to decipher the nu-merical data encoded in the pits on the surface of the disc. First, a laser diode pro-jects a thin, continuous beam of red light. This is typically a small, low-powered laser that is perfectly safe and rela-tively inexpensive to manu-facture—nothing like the powerful lasers used for cut-ting or other industrial appli-cations. Laser light, when passed through lenses, stays focused and does not scatter as does regular white light.

A set of mirrors and lenses focuses the beam with pin-

In the few years since its introduction, the laser pickup has been reduced in size and made easier and cheaper to manufacture.

point accuracy on the disc, directly in the center of the track being read. The beam is reflected off the metallic surface and directed into a *photodetector cell* which decodes the data and transmits them to the next stage.

When the laser beam strikes a flat place between pits, called a *land*, the light is reflected back as a sharp beam, with little loss of intensity. When the beam

strikes a pit, something different happens to the light. Because the reflective surface of the pit is offset from the land by about ¼ of a wavelength of the laser light, the light reflected from a land travels about ½ of a wavelength farther than the light reflected from a pit. This half-wavelength offset, or *phase difference*, between the two types of reflections results in *phase cancellation* of much of the beam's light energy. The phase difference causes most of the light's energy to be cancelled out when it encounters a pit.

Thus, as the track of pits and lands passes above the laser beam, the reflected light varies in strength. When the beam encounters a land, the light is reflected at full strength. When it encounters a pit, the strength of the reflected light beam is diminished. The result is a constantly flickering reflection, in which pulses correspond to the pits and lands on the disc.

The reflected light is directed through another lens which focuses it on the photodetector, a unit that converts the pulses of light into digital data that can be used by the computer circuits. The photodetector is composed of several *photodiodes*, sensitive optical switches that respond to light by giving off an electrical current.

As the track of pits passes above the laser beam, the photodetector creates a binary bit stream that represents the varying pattern of pits and lands on the disc. This flow of digital data is then passed along to the data decoding system where it is transformed into an audio signal.

One of the most remarkable attributes of the CD system is the incredibly small scale at which the data are written on the disc. The spiral track of pits is only 1.6 micrometers wide—about ⅟₆₀th the diameter of a human hair. The laser beam must come to a focus in an area no more than 1 micrometer wide and remain focused while the disc spins at speeds up to 500 rpm.

Because the data are read by a laser beam, no part of the player ever touches the encoded music on the disc. This is one of the primary reasons for both the long life and the noise-free playing of the Compact Disc.

The Servo System

The photodetector, in addition to translating the laser beam's information into the digital bit stream, helps maintain the proper focus and tracking of the laser. It sends signals to the CD controller which first determines the necessary focus and tracking corrections, and then sends commands to the *servomechanisms*, or servos. These small electrical devices make constant minute adjustments to the position of the laser pickup to keep the beam in focus and on track.

Because a disc cannot be made perfectly flat, the precise position of the disc surface above the laser pickup varies as the disc rotates. Proper focus is essential for the photodiode to distinguish the digital bit stream coming from the disc. If the focus strays, the phase cancellation between the light reflected from the pits and lands becomes less precise, resulting in a signal that cannot be interpreted by the photodiode.

To maintain the exact focus, the reflected beam passes through a cylindrical lens (in some player designs) before it enters the photodetector. If the focus strays, the cylindri-cal lens causes the beam to deform into an elliptical shape. The photodetector senses this change and generates an *auto-focus* signal to a servo that moves the laser pickup either closer to or farther from the disc's surface as required. Specifically, the laser must stay focused within a tolerance of 2 micrometers. (Remember, a human hair is about 100 micrometers in diameter.)

The proper tracking of the spiral of pits is essential to creating an accurate stream of data from the CD. To keep the laser beam centered on the track, the photodiode measures changes in intensity of the reflected light. If the beam strays to one side of the track, the proportion of reflected light will be greater, and the photodiode generates a tracking error signal that triggers the servos to move the laser pickup to the left or right to bring the beam back on track.

Both the auto-focus and auto-tracking systems operate

on what is termed *closed-loop feedback*. This is a self-correcting system in which any movement that strays from proper focus or tracking generates a correction signal that automatically moves the pickup in the direction to correct for the deviation. As you listen to your CD, the servo system is constantly correcting the position of the laser pickup to keep it in focus and on track within incredibly tiny tolerances.

The Data Decoding System

Just as the original analog signal was encoded for digital storage at the recording and manufacturing stage, so must the digital data be decoded back into analog signals for playback. Transforming the flickering of the reflected laser light into sound is accomplished by a sophisticated system of electronic circuits within the player.

When the digital audio was encoded on the disc, the data were modulated by adding bits to enable the laser in the player to properly interpret and read the data. The first step in decoding the signal from the photodetector is demodulation, whereby the data are restored to their original bit structure. Additional decoding circuits rearrange the data, returning them to their original sequence and removing now unnecessary organizational information. The digital data stream is further processed to reveal playing-time information which is then presented by the time display on the player.

In the next step, error-correction coding circuits (ECC) attempt to compensate for any data (audio samples) that might be obscured on a scratched or defective disc. (The process of error protection, in which check codes and parity bits are added to the data, is explained in Chapter 2.) When the data on the disc are decoded in the player, circuits in the player use the check codes and parity bits to try to detect and correct erroneous data. Unlike an LP or a tape, where missing information will cause a click or a dropout, the CD can use its digital power to effectively conceal an error.

The ECC circuits have three ways to deal with errors detected in the data. The system first tries to reconstruct the data using the check codes and parity bits. The ECC system is capable of completely recreating all data lost in a scratch or defect of up to 1/10th of an inch long.

If the disc defect or scratch obscures more data, the interpolation circuits then try to *interpolate*, or fill in, the data between two adjacent audio samples. Because the data are in digital form, the player calculates the value of the audio data as an average of the samples before and after the error. Interpolation will handle errors caused by as much as a 1/4-inch loss of data on the disc.

When the error is too extensive for interpolation, the player simply *mutes* the output until a valid data flow is resumed. This doesn't necessarily mean that you hear silence during muted errors. The human hearing system cannot ordinarily detect a muted silence in music shorter than $\frac{1}{15}$th to $\frac{1}{20}$th of a second, thus giving the player considerable leeway in dealing with errors in the audio data while continuing to deliver sound.

From this point onward, the data go through the stages of demultiplexing, digital-to-analog conversion, and output filtering as described in Chapter 2.

The Control and Display System

The CD controller is the computer, or microprocessor, which governs the functioning of all the systems in the player, managing the flow of data throughout. You might think of the controller as the equivalent of our higher brain functions—

keeping all of the input and output systems working as a coherent whole.

The controller compares the synchronization pulses from the data stream with an internal quartz clock and sends a signal to the disc drive motor to speed up or slow down, as necessary. It also receives the auto-focus and auto-tracking signals from the photodetector and, in response, generates the signals that keep the laser pickup in proper position. Perhaps most importantly, the controller manages the flow of digital information from the photodetector to the processing circuits where it is decoded and converted into an analog of the original sound. The controller also provides the interface with the controls and displays on the exterior of the player. It senses which buttons are pushed and causes the system to respond appropriately. It then modifies the display of information on the front panel of the player accordingly.

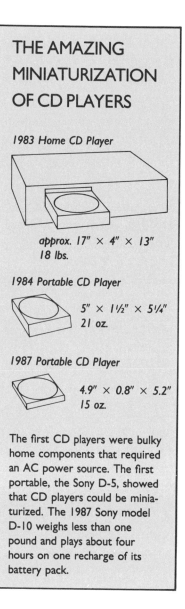

THE AMAZING MINIATURIZATION OF CD PLAYERS

1983 Home CD Player

approx. 17" × 4" × 13"
18 lbs.

1984 Portable CD Player

5" × 1½" × 5¼"
21 oz.

1987 Portable CD Player

4.9" × 0.8" × 5.2"
15 oz.

The first CD players were bulky home components that required an AC power source. The first portable, the Sony D-5, showed that CD players could be miniaturized. The 1987 Sony model D-10 weighs less than one pound and plays about four hours on one recharge of its battery pack.

TECHNICAL SPECIFICATIONS

All CD players function in the same basic manner described above. The disc spins, the laser reads the data in the pits, and electronic circuitry translates the data into sound. It's all standardized in accordance with the Philips/Sony specifications for the Compact Disc Digital Audio system, allowing any disc to play in any player.

But even though all CD players meet this basic standard, exactly how the technology is implemented varies from one model to the next. As a result, the audio *performance* of CD players varies. Many use components that exceed the minimum requirements of the CD system. To gauge the relative merits of CD players, a series of technical specifications have been developed that allow you to compare the players' measured audio performance.

Technical specifications, or "specs" as they are commonly referred to, may appear in both the manufacturer's brochures and magazine reviews. Technical specifications are laboratory measurements of various aspects of a CD player's audio output. Audio engineers connect a player to sophisticated electronic equipment to test the quality of its performance.

Using test specs to distinguish between Compact Disc players can be difficult even for those who know how to interpret them. Compared to the degree of variance between phonograph specifications, CD players seem to show hardly any differences at all. This is one reason it is commonly said that most CD players sound the same. Even the most discerning listener may have difficulty detecting significant differences with the naked ear.

Still, with a little familiarization, technical specifications can provide useful evidence on which to base judgments about the relative merits of players. While the jargon used to impart technical specifications may look formidable, it is simply telling you what you can expect to hear in the performance of a piece of audio gear.

Two units of measurement pervade most audio specifications. Frequency, expressed in hertz or kilohertz, was explained in Chapter 2. Frequency is an absolute measurement. If a tone is 440 Hz, it oscillates 440 times a second.

The other unit of measure is the *decibel*, abbreviated dB, which is a relative measurement. The decibel measures *differences* in loudness, usually between a reference signal and a measured signal. A difference of 3 dB in loudness is about the smallest change that can be readily discerned in the playback of music. Also, it takes an increase of 10 dB to double the perceived loudness of a sound.

Technical specifications address two basic points: 1) whether all the sounds are equally represented, and 2) how cleanly and purely they are reproduced. The five most common specs included for CD players are listed below, each with a brief explanation.

Frequency Response

The *frequency response* of a CD player tells how accurately and consistently it reproduces the full range of audible frequencies. Frequency response is measured in terms of the maximum deviation of a signal level, in plus or minus decibels, at any point along the frequency spectrum. This information is often shown in graphical form.

The frequency response of LPs and tapes often deviates several dB in frequencies above 10 kHz, and this occasionally results in higher frequencies not being reproduced at all. On most CD players, any tone between 20 Hz and 20 kHz will be reproducible and should vary no more than $+/- 1.0$ dB.

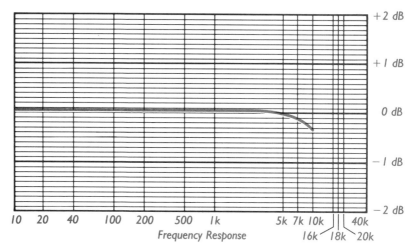

Frequency Response

Recommended Specification: Frequency response from 20 Hz to 20 kHz, with no more than 0.5 dB deviance.

S/N Ratio

The *signal-to-noise (S/N) ratio* measures the difference in level between the *system noise* within an audio component and the loudest signal it can produce without noticeable *distortion*.

You have probably experienced both noise and distortion even if you didn't recognize them as such. Distortion is the harsh fuzziness of tone you get if you boost your

Frequency response is measured as a deviation from 0 dB across the range of audible frequencies (20 Hz to 20 kHz). This curve shows a frequency response that begins to drop at about 7 kHz and reaches a value of -0.5 dB at 20 kHz, an acceptable performance for a CD player.

system's volume to its upper limits while listening to a recording. Noise is the sound you will hear if you do the same while no audio signal is being input to the system. It is the hiss or hum produced by the electronics of the system itself.

The S/N ratio also determines the unit's *dynamic*

range, the difference, in decibels, between the quietest recorded signal level a player or disc can produce and the loudest. CD performance in this respect is uniformly impressive. The format specifications for CD-Audio allow for at least 90 dB in dynamic range from any player. This means the player can reproduce signals 90 dB above its softest signal without distorting.

Since a quiet room in a typical household has a background threshold of around 40 dB, any sound the player produces below 40 dB will be inaudible to the listener. Thus, 40 dB might be considered the softest threshold of sound the player can reproduce. With a 90 dB dynamic range, therefore, a player is capable of producing sounds of around 130 dB (40 dB + 90 dB) without distorting. Since the upper limit capabilities of most standard amplifiers and speakers rarely exceed 125

dB, this means that most CD players will utilize the full capabilities of almost any current consumer stereo system.

The higher the S/N ratio the better. Most players have an S/N ratio of over 90 dB, which results in a very quiet background for the sound from the disc.

Published specifications often include an *A-weighted* value for S/N ratio. This measurement uses a scale that compensates for the auditory characteristics of the human ear. A-weighting usually produces higher values than an unweighted S/N ratio. Since you cannot compare the unweighted S/N ratio of one player with the A-weighted ratio of another, most manufacturers and reviewers now list both. The A-weighted ratio is most useful since it more accurately reflects what you hear. *Recommended Specification*: S/N Ratio at least 95 dB (unweighted). S/N Ratio at least 100 dB (A-weighted).

Total Harmonic Distortion (THD)

In most audio components, the electronic circuitry adds distortion to the signal in the form of *harmonics*, or related overtones. For example, a basic 440-Hz tone would have harmonic overtones at integer multiples of its frequency—880 Hz, 1320 Hz, 1760 Hz, and so forth.

You may not notice moderate levels of this type of distortion, since it is masked by the natural harmonics of the instruments in the recordings. However, the distortion becomes more audible with single-frequency tones produced by instruments such as flutes or synthesizers.

The rating is given as the percentage of THD + Noise in the signal at various dB levels, and most CD players rarely exceed .005 percent. *Recommended Specification*: THD + Noise no more than .005 percent at 1 kHz.

Intermodulation Distortion

Another type of distortion added by the electronics is termed *intermodulation distortion*, or IM distortion. This distortion takes place when multiple tones in the recorded signal interact to form unwanted tones whose frequencies are equal to the sum or difference of the frequencies of the original tones. For instance, a 200-Hz tone and a 750-Hz tone produce a sum tone of 950 Hz and a difference tone of 550 Hz. Since these tones are not harmonically related to the original tones, IM distortion tends to be more annoying than THD.

Like THD, IM distortion is listed as the percentage present in the signal at various levels. While IM may be higher than THD in most players, it still should rarely exceed .01 percent.

Recommended Specification: IM distortion no more than .01 percent.

Channel Separation

Channel separation measures the degree to which the left and right channels are isolated from one another. Interference from the other channel is termed *crosstalk*. The level of crosstalk between channels becomes unnoticeable at channel separations in the 30-dB level. Most CD players have excellent separation and suffer from almost no crosstalk. Ratings in the upper 90-dB range are typical, which means almost total isolation between left and right channel signals.

Recommended Specification: Channel separation at least 95 dB at 1 kHz.

PERFORMANCE FEATURES

A CD player contains a myriad of electronic circuits, the overall quality of which affects a player's measured technical specifications. Several specialized types of circuits are appearing with increasing frequency in many CD players. Although primarily designed to improve the quality of the sound, these performance features are not necessarily reflected in a player's technical specifications. Nevertheless, they play an important role in distinguishing player models.

Digital Filtering

One example is the use of digital filters instead of the analog filters used in the decoding systems of many earlier players. Filtering of the sound is necessary to remove unwanted high frequencies generated by the electronics.

Analog filtering takes place after the signal has been converted from digital to analog. This uses a circuit that operates in the analog realm, relying on its electrical properties to effectively filter the higher frequencies. Analog filters can result in erratic performance since they are difficult to manufacture with consistent quality.

Digital filtering takes place before the signal is converted to analog. Digital filters operate much more reliably than their analog counterparts. They are efficient at removing frequencies far above the audible hearing range. The digital filters found in some CD players always use a technique called *oversampling*.

An oversampling filter boosts the frequency of the extraneous overtones so they can be efficiently removed by "gentle" analog filters. An oversampling filter typically uses a sampling rate two or four times the original 44.1-kHz input sampling rate (88.2 kHz or 176.4 kHz). This does not mean that the frequency response is doubled. It simply means that the entire signal is multiplied so that proper analog filtering can take place.

In general, digital filters, when combined with over-sampling, contribute to a more consistent level of quality in a CD player's audio output.

Dual Digital-to-Analog Converters

The sound may also be improved by having two digital-to-analog converters. The CD system is designed so that a single DAC will suffice, by alternating the left and right channel output every $\frac{1}{150}$th of a second. This introduces a $\frac{1}{75}$th-second delay between the two channels. Dual DACs eliminate this channel switching, restoring the original synchronization of the left and right output channels. Considering the speed of sound in air, a $\frac{1}{75}$th-second delay is the equivalent of moving one speaker a distance of less than one inch either closer or farther away. As a result, this effect of a single DAC is practically imperceptible.

Error-Correction Circuitry

One characteristic you rarely notice is the quality of a player's error-correction coding (ECC) circuitry. This factor may not be so important when you play a new disc that has not been scratched. But as your CD collection gets more use, the discs will inevitably acquire some scratches. Players with higher-quality ECC circuitry will be able to play these discs with less sound interpolation and muting and with fewer tracking errors. Unfortunately, there is not much you can do to evaluate a player's ECC and tracking performance, other than to read reviews in which the reviewer has subjected the player to a special test disc that measures a player's ability to handle various degrees of disc defects.

Three-Beam Laser Pickup

Another performance feature often mentioned by stereo salespeople is the *three-beam laser pickup*. This does not mean there are three lasers in the player, but rather the main beam is split, creating two secondary beams on either side of the primary beam. These secondary beams are focused on the edges of pits in adjacent tracks, and are reflected into separate sensors in the main photodetector to check for tracking of the primary beam. Most critics agree that three-beam systems don't necessarily track any better than single-beam systems. Furthermore, tracking performance is also affected by the quality of the circuits of the servo system and the general construction of the player's chassis.

Access Time

The disc drive motor and the mechanism that moves the laser pickup affect *access time*, or how long it takes to get from one portion of the disc to another. Early players took as much as six or eight seconds to traverse the inch and a half between the inner and outer edges of the pro-

gramming area. This has been greatly improved, with end-to-end access times of less than one second now available. A faster access time means less waiting between tracks of a programmed sequence.

HIGH-END AUDIO

The search for the perfect CD player has led a few manufacturers to some rarefied heights. At the extreme is the Accuphase DP80/DC81, a two-unit CD player that costs a mere $7000. (Yes, that does include a remote control.) The DC 81 houses the disc drive and laser unit, while the DP 80 module contains the electronics and signal processing circuitry. This approach virtually eliminates the noise and distortion that may result from interplay between the elec-

tronics and drive mechanisms in most players.

Further improvements in sound quality can be found in other high-priced players, especially those using top-grade components in the circuits that process the audio after it has been converted into an analog signal. A few players even use the older technology of vacuum tubes, instead of the transistors that have generally replaced them, to amplify the sound in its final stages before leaving the player. Some audiophiles claim that vacuum-tube circuitry creates a "warmer" sound.

Improved circuit design in some players may produce cleaner signals. For example, separate power sources for the digital and analog components in the system are said to help isolate spurious signals that could interfere ▶

with the quality of the sound. Other players use fiber optics to transmit signals from the digital components to the analog circuitry, thereby almost eliminating electrical noise.

If you're a fanatic about top-quality sound, some high-end players offer extra processing of the digital audio. For example, some Carver players include a Digital Time Lens, a selectable circuit designed to correct problems stemming from poorly recorded discs. A DBX model offers Digital Audio Impact Recovery (DAIR), which boosts certain audio frequencies allegedly to help recreate the acoustics of a live performance.

Additional digital signal processing is available with add-on components that allow you to add spaciousness to the room ambience by filtering, compression, and phase manipulation of the signal. These devices typically function as a middle stage between the output of the player and the input to the stereo system. For this reason, some players now have jacks on the rear panel for direct digital output. This gives you the option of diverting the undecoded digital signal from the player, prior to conversion to analog, into one of these digital processing components.

Physically induced noise can be a problem as well. For example, very slight vibrations in the player chassis itself, caused by resonance from the electronics and the room sound, may cause unwanted noise in the signal. Some players alleviate the problem by shock-mounting the disc drive mechanism.

Most of these high-end audio enhancements carry a hefty price tag. And their audible value may sometimes be far outweighed by the pure emotion of owner satisfaction. Make sure you examine the E/C ratio (ego-to-checkbook ratio) of any high-end player before you buy.

CHAPTER 4

Push-Button Music: CD-Player Features

Most CD players sound uniformly good as a result of the strict set of standards that Philips and Sony license to hardware makers. Even experts sometimes have trouble discerning the subtle differences between various models. That is why both manufacturers and consumers concentrate on specific control and convenience features to distinguish one player from another.

If you're a first-time CD buyer, an understanding of these features can help prepare you for a wise purchase. Or, if you're an owner interested in replacing or augmenting your present equipment, knowing the specific details about the features can help you make sense of new product ideas on the market. Most of the features offered on CD players can be roughly divided into these three categories:

- Basic features: those required for simple access and playback of music on the CD, found on virtually all CD players.
- Convenience features: those which are not needed for good sound or basic use, but, through added convenience, distinguish one CD model from another, usually with a corresponding price differential.
- Special features: extras often related to a player's special use as a portable or car model, or its ability to handle multiple discs or outputs.

Of course, not all of these features are necessary for optimum enjoyment of your player. You can find many models for less than $200, offering only the most basic functions, and, in most cases, performing every bit as well for casual listening as models costing much more.

This chapter covers the range of features and explains what they do for you. Armed with this understanding, you can go on to the next chapter for help in narrowing your choices and making an intelligent buying decision.

BASIC FEATURES

Power Switch

Every player has a power switch to turn the machine on and off. Even with such a basic feature you'll find variations that may surprise you.

If the power is turned on while a disc is in the drawer,

Most home players include a display of track number and playing time and controls for operating the disc drawer, selecting tracks, and programming a sequence of tracks. Useful options include a headphone jack and remote control.

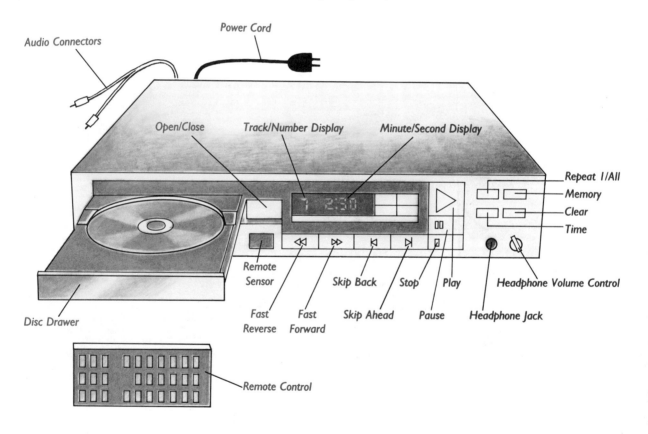

Audio Connectors

Power Cord

Open/Close

Track/Number Display

Minute/Second Display

Repeat 1/All
Memory
Clear
Time

Remote Sensor

Skip Back Stop Play

Headphone Volume Control

Fast Reverse Fast Forward Skip Ahead Pause Headphone Jack

Disc Drawer

Remote Control

some players automatically begin playing the disc. This feature has hidden advantages. If you hook such a player to a timer switch (the kind that turns your lamps on when you're on vacation), you can wake up to your favorite CD. Just leave the disc in the drawer and set the timer before you turn in. When the machine receives power, it will play the disc. Some machines have a switch so you can select this option, since you may not want to have the disc begin playing every time your system is turned on.

Some players provide an extra AC outlet on the rear panel into which you may plug the power cord of another component, such as a cassette deck or an FM tuner. The outlet is configured as either *switched* or *unswitched*, indicating whether or not the player must be switched on for power to be in the outlet. If you want to operate the other component when the player might not be turned on, you would choose a model with an unswitched outlet.

Disc Drawer

Every player has some type of button or switch that opens and closes the disc compartment. On almost all of today's home models, this compartment is a tray or drawer that slides out to receive the disc. One exception is the Bang & Olufsen CDX, which has a top-loading disc drive. You open the top cover by hand and set the disc directly on the disc spindle. This design has proved only moderately popular. Although it means less chance of a drawer malfunction, there is more exposure of the sensitive disc drive and laser unit mechanisms.

Players offer various systems for opening and closing the sliding disc drawer. A gentle push on some drawers causes them to close. However, most require you to press an OPEN/CLOSE button somewhere on the front panel. This may be located directly on the drawer itself, which can prove inconvenient if you try to press the button while the drawer is in motion. In some cases, closing the drawer causes the disc to begin to play.

Most portable models don't have motorized disc drawers. Instead, they have a manually operated hinged door which covers the disc compartment. This design usually offers the most trouble-free operation considering the rough treatment portable units may receive.

PLAY Button

Pressing the PLAY button causes the player to begin playing the disc in the drawer. The laser pickup moves to track 1, or the first programmed track, and begins play. A CD may have up to 99 tracks, each of which usually corresponds to a song or passage of music on the disc.

Typically, pressing PLAY will also cause an extended

disc drawer to close since play cannot begin until this happens. In a few machines, pressing PLAY can turn the power on when the player is off. Many PLAY buttons have an indicator light to show you when the machine is playing a disc.

The PLAY button may have additional control functions. The Onkyo DX-320, for instance, features a "smart" PLAY button, a small indentation in the front panel with a light sensor at its center. When you touch the indentation, the CD controller checks to see if a disc is in the tray. If it finds a disc, play begins; if not, it extends the drawer for a disc to be inserted.

Some PLAY buttons, when pressed during play, will return the laser to the beginning of the current track, while others return to the first track. Others simply don't respond if the machine is already playing a disc.

PAUSE Button

The PAUSE button is familiar to cassette-deck owners. It allows you to pause the music and then resume play where it left off when

Although specific styles of controls and names of buttons may vary among manufacturers, most CD player controls are very easy to operate. Basic displays show track number and playing time, while complex displays show status of repeat modes, programmed sequence, and various time information about the disc.

PAUSE was pressed. Usually PAUSE is a separate button that alternately pauses and resumes play. In some cases, however, the PLAY button itself doubles as the PAUSE button.

Another pause option is referred to as *auto-pause*. Activating this feature causes the player to automatically pause at the end of each track. You must then press PAUSE or PLAY for the program to continue. This is a useful feature for selective listening.

STOP Button

The STOP button causes the player to stop rotating the disc and to return the laser pickup to its initial position. For this reason it is referred to on some players as a RESET or RETURN button. Pressing STOP usually cancels any programmed sequence in memory. Hitting this button accidentally can mean having to go through the programming routine again. Some players have a CANCEL button for cancelling the programmed sequence, allowing you to use the STOP button during playback of a programmed sequence.

Track Selection

The array of track selection buttons varies widely among players. Minimal-design players accomplish the task with a few simple multipurpose buttons. Other players employ numeric keypads in combination with task-specific buttons to control track selection.

Virtually all players have two basic *track selection* buttons—one for moving forward to the next track, the other for moving backward to the previous one. These track selection buttons are variously labeled as FORWARD and REVERSE, or SKIP, and are often marked with single or double arrows pointing to a vertical line. They cause the laser pickup to move along sequentially from track to track in either direction. If held down, the pickup usually continues to move through the tracks. In some models, these same buttons may be used to select tracks when programming the player.

The FAST FORWARD and FAST REVERSE buttons are often marked with extra forward or backward arrows, or the letters FF and FR. If the player features *audible scanning*, you will be able to hear the music on the track moving by at an increased rate of speed. This makes it much easier to find specific points within a selection. Some players feature two-speed scanning. This is typically accomplished with two sets of forward and reverse buttons, with each set offering a different scanning speed. Others offer two-speed scanning using a single pair of buttons. When you first depress the button, the player scans at its slower speed. If you continue holding it down, after the first few seconds, the player moves into a faster scanning rate.

Players with numeric keypads allow you to key in the specific track numbers you want to hear. This is a useful feature that makes "push-button" music a practical reality on a CD player. Tracks selected with a keypad may either be played immediately or stored in memory for programmed playback. Remote control units, which often duplicate many track selection functions of the front panel, are covered later in this chapter.

Index Selection

On some discs, tracks are subdivided into smaller segments marked by *index points* within the track. Many players have buttons to allow you to move forward or backward through such a track from one index point to another. Index points are most often used in long classical pieces to mark succes-sive movements or passages that aren't long enough to merit separate tracks. A disc's index points (if any) are usually delineated in the printed booklet in the jewel box or on the disc's label.

For example, London Record's recording of the Montreal Symphony performing Stravinsky's *The Rite of Spring* has one track each for Parts I and II of the ballet, for a total of 35 minutes and 40 seconds of playing time. The disc's 13 index points within these two tracks delineate segments as short as 44 seconds. INDEX buttons make it easy to go directly to any of these specific points instead of scanning with the less precise FAST FORWARD and FAST REVERSE buttons.

Display

The lighted display window keeps you informed about the status of play, material on the disc, and time information. Since displays provide perhaps the most direct user contact, a great amount of attention goes into their design and the results may be very innovative. The light sources may be any of the familiar glows typically found on electronic gear—for example, greenish fluorescent light, red light-emitting diodes, or silvery liquid-crystal displays, as well as other colors to differentiate information on the display. The size and brightness of the display affect its readability from the varying distances. You might want to experiment with different displays in the sales room to find one to your liking.

Virtually every display shows the track number and elapsed playing time of the track being played. (Many also show the index number.) This is basically all you need to tell where you are in a disc.

But other information can be helpful. For example,

when you first insert a disc in some players, the display shows the total number of tracks and total playing time of the disc. As the disc plays, you can alternate the time display to show remaining time on the disc—including remaining time in a programmed sequence.

Various information about the mode of operation may also be shown. Most displays have some form of Play, Pause, and Stop indicator, either in the display window or on the buttons themselves. Data about the repeat mode—whether you have specified repeat of a single track or the entire disc—may also show up in the display. Some players even have an indicator to show you whether a disc is in the drawer.

Program information, indicating how many tracks are left and/or their sequence, is typically shown in some manner on the display. Sony's Music Calendar dis-

play shows the total range of tracks on the disc (up to 20) and then blanks them out as they are played.

CONVENIENCE FEATURES

While the basic features listed above are found on virtually all players, you may not always find the following features. Since they are not absolutely essential to the operation of the player, they are offered for your added convenience. Certain of these, however, such as the repeat and program functions, are rapidly becoming standard options because of their wide popularity.

Repeat Functions

One of the unique capabilities of the CD is the repeat function, which allows you to replay portions of the disc in many different ways. The full range of options includes:

repeat one track, repeat all tracks, repeat the program, repeat a specified segment of the disc, or random play. Players may have all, some, or none of these abilities—it varies widely among manufacturers.

Repeat functions are selected with one or more REPEAT buttons. For example, a player may have separate buttons for selecting REPEAT ONE, REPEAT ALL, and REPEAT A–B. The latter function repeats any portion of the disc from point A to point B—a process called *loop repeat*, or *A–B repeat*. This may be of marginal use to the average listener, but can be very handy for musicians who want to take advantage of the CD's access capabilities to learn material from the disc.

In sparser designs, a single REPEAT button can act as a toggle switch, letting you choose the desired repeat mode as shown on the display. Pressing the STOP button in most cases cancels the repeat pattern which has been set up. Other players, however, may require a specific action such as pressing a CLEAR or CANCEL button to do so.

Programmability

The degree and flexibility of the programming function is an area where you will find highly competitive design among player manufacturers. Almost all players are programmable to some degree. One area of distinction is the number of tracks that can be programmed into the player's memory at any one time. Most allow up to 15 tracks, although the number ranges from as few as 8 to as many as 99 tracks.

How you program the tracks varies from machine to machine, but it's usually pretty simple. A common method involves a single MEMORY or PROGRAM button used in conjunction with the track selection buttons. For example, suppose you want to hear only tracks 5, 7, and 11 on a disc in your player. To program that sequence, first press the MEMORY button. The player responds with some indication on the display that it is ready to be programmed. The next step is to use the track selection buttons to skip to track 5 as shown on the display. Press MEMORY again to store track 5 as the first selection in the program. Then select tracks 7 and 11 in the same way. Finally, press PLAY to start playback of the programmed sequence.

More expensive machines may have a numeric keypad, either on the player or on the remote, that you can use to select tracks for the programmed sequence. Once you begin program play, some of the basic functions such as pause and repeat may continue to operate on the entire program.

Remote Control

Many types of remote control devices are available and come as standard equipment with many players. Some models, however, offer a remote as an optional accessory. If you don't particularly care for this feature, you can choose a player without one and save between $50 and $100.

Most remote control units are wireless, working on infrared beams of light. This means you have to aim the remote at the front panel of the player. A very few come with wired remotes. Though they tend to be more awkward and have proved less popular, they nonetheless offer some distinct advantages. At least one wired model, for instance, offers a small display panel on the remote unit—possible due to the connection through which to send track and timing information to the remote unit.

The better remotes duplicate most, if not all, of the functions found on the front control panel of the player (play, pause, track selection,

This remote control has a numeric keypad for easy selection of track numbers.

A volume control for a headphone jack is essential for adjusting the output level.

fast forward, fast reverse, stop). In some cases, they offer extra functions not found even on the front panel. For example, the remote may have a keypad while the player may not.

If you're stretched out on your couch and want to adjust the volume on a passage of a disc, most players offer only one choice: get up and change the volume control on your amplifier. If this seems a real inconvenience, you might want to consider one of the players offering a volume control on the remote unit. Although you

typically can't use the remote to turn the volume all the way up or down, there's usually enough range to accommodate normal listening situations.

Some players incorporate a beep indicator that causes the player to emit an audible beep to indicate when the player has received a signal from the remote. This feature can usually be switched on or off.

Remotes may even be integrated with other components to offer one-point control of VCRs, TVs, cassettes, and receivers as well. Kyocera's Full System Remote Control and RCA's Digital Command Center are examples.

Headphone Jack

A number of home players offer an output jack for headphone listening, but it is by no means a standard feature. Some models with a headphone jack also offer a variable-volume-level control for the headphone signal. If you

enjoy headphone listening, a volume control can be very useful. Chapter 5 provides guidelines on choosing headphones for CD equipment.

SPECIAL FEATURES

This section reflects the considerable effort which has gone into expansion of CD-player design. Every round of new product introductions reveals innovative ideas intended to push player capability beyond current limits. This may range from multiple-disc capacity to improved electronics to compatibility with add-on equipment available in the future. Once again, such features are not necessary for ordinary enjoyment of the Compact Disc. But if you find gadgetry irresistible, the list of new temptations seems to stretch endlessly.

Multiple-Disc Changers

The CD multiple-disc feature is appearing on more and more players, since users find it very convenient to have access to several discs at a time. Machines such as the Mitsubishi DP-409 and the Sony CDP-C10 offer multidisc cartridges that hold up to ten discs. Other models have cartridges holding five, six, or eight CDs. The style and design of the cartridges vary but they generally involve preloading the discs, then inserting the cartridge into a slot in the front panel of the player. Selections may be programmed for continuous play of a number of tracks from any or all discs.

Extra cartridges may be purchased so that your entire

The cartridge for the Sony Disc-Jockey™ CD player holds 10 discs, each of which may be accessed within seconds from the controls or as part of a programmed sequence.

library can be stored in cartridges. Some players offer an optional single-disc drawer that may be used alternately with the discs in the cartridge. This means you can play a single disc without having to first load it in a cartridge.

A new type of multidisc player holds five discs in a platter that slides out like a

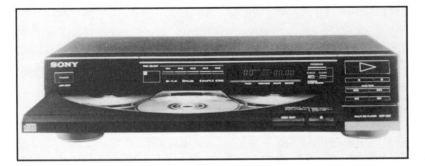

The Sony CDP-C5F DiscJockey™ features a platter arrangement that makes it easy to identify and change any of the five discs.

drawer. This arrangement makes it very easy to see which discs you want to change in the platter.

Several models from Sony and Nikko take this concept even further with built-in racks that can hold up to 60 discs, resulting in a potential of 75 hours of continuous random selection playback. Some of these units can further be linked together to create a player chain capable of accessing up to 240 discs. Although these models cost several thousand dollars, you can expect to see the price drop as their popularity grows.

Music Memory

A few players recall programmed sequences on different discs even during subsequent listening sessions. The Magnavox CDB650 offers this unique programming feature under the name Favorite Track Selection (FTS). FTS allows you to preprogram up to 785 tracks for dozens of individual

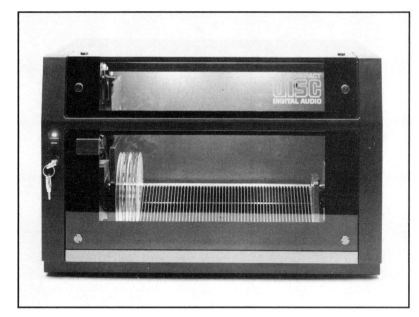

discs. The machine stores the programs in memory along with a disc recognition code. Even after the machine has been turned off, the program remains in memory so that when you next put the disc in, the player recognizes the disc and calls up its personal program.

Shuffle Play

The Sony "Shuffle Play" feature is a type of programmed playback in which

If you can afford its several-thousand-dollar price tag, the Sony CDK-006 60-disc changer will give you more than seventy hours worth of music at the touch of a few buttons.

the player itself selects the order of the tracks, mixing them randomly. This is useful for adding surprise interest to CDs that have become too familiar and overused. If you tire easily of predictability, this feature may help you avoid the routine presentation of your discs.

Auto Scan

This feature is beginning to appear with more regularity. It may be marketed under other trade names, such as Music Scan. In this play mode, the machine plays perhaps the first 10 seconds of a track, then moves on to the next. It is primarily useful as a tool for previewing material on unfamiliar discs.

Random Access by Time within Track

This feature allows you to directly access points of time within a track. For example, if you don't want to hear the first 1 minute and 55 seconds on track 2, you can program the player to begin track 2 at the 1:55 point, thus sparing yourself the wait.

Subcode Output

This connector on the back of some CD players has not yet received much practical application. It was designed to output song lyrics or accompanying still pictures stored in the *subcode* of a disc. Connection to a subcode decoder unit would display the information on your TV screen.

No decoder units have yet been marketed in the U.S. Only a handful of subcode discs have been released, and in the absence of the extra decoder hardware, these do nothing more than play audio. The Japanese market is the only one so far to put subcode data to any commercial use. Japan's popular sing-along nightclubs, called *karaoke* bars, use the subcode to display lyrics from the disc on TV monitors. The appearance of players with this connector implies an eventual application to this extended use. However, most manufacturers now believe that the subcode approach will be made obsolete by the *interactive* CD format described in Chapter 10.

CD/Cassette-Deck Combination

A CD player with a cassette deck built into the same unit holds a certain appeal for many since it facilitates the recording of CD material onto tape. Home taping of LPs is firmly established because it provides a tape copy of favorite music that can be used in a portable or auto cassette deck. It also saves wear and tear on the LP. It's uncertain how popular CD taping will become, since unlike LPs, CDs are as portable as cassettes. Furthermore, CDs don't wear out. And a taped copy of a CD reintroduces noise such as tape hiss into the quiet of the digital domain.

CD/Videodisc Player Combination

What has proved to be a more popular combination unit is one that plays both CDs and LaserVision videodiscs. Pioneer was the first on the market with their CLD-900 model, but a number of other units have since appeared. The LaserVision videodisc format stores full-motion color video with optional digital soundtracks.

The TEAC AD-7 combination CD player and cassette deck. This unit makes it easy to tape the material from the CD onto a cassette tape.

The 12-inch discs hold up to an hour of video on each side; the 7-inch variety contains 20 minutes per side. The LaserVision format has grown in popularity since RCA's discontinuation of its SelectaVision videodisc format.

Both LaserVision and Compact Disc use a laser to read the program material. The engineering challenge was to create one machine that could handle the different-sized discs, electronics, rotational speeds, and types of data stored on each format. The combination of the Compact Disc and video has been carried a step further with the new CD-Video standard discussed in Chapter 10.

Other Special Features

Another option that appeals mainly to buyers interested in making cassette copies of their CDs is the Auto Space (or Auto Silence) capability found on certain models. This feature causes a three- to four-second interval of silence to be automatically inserted between the taped copies of the CD tracks. If you have the type of cassette deck that looks for the next song by cueing on the silences between cuts, a three- to four-second pause may be necessary for a silence to be detected. Since some CD players move between tracks in as little as one second, this interval may be ignored by the auto-search on a cassette player.

For the CD disc jockey in you, there is Toshiba's XR-V22 with two separate disc drawers and a single laser pickup that can read discs in either drawer. To play DJ, put a disc in the first drawer and begin playing a track. While you wait for that track to end, load the next disc in the second drawer. When the track on the disc in the first drawer ends, you can go right to a track on the second disc. You can alternate between songs on different discs for as long as you like, with a break of only a few seconds between songs.

Players such as the Nu-mark CD9000 and the Nikko NCD-600 include variable pitch and tempo controls. These controls let you either raise or lower the pitch or speed up or slow down the tempo of a song. Unlike similar controls found on some cassette decks and turntables, altering the pitch on a CD player does not affect the tempo, and vice versa. Performers who want to play or sing along can use this feature to match their voice or instrument to the pitch and tempo of the recording. Musicians and educators, as well as the Japanese karaoke devotees, find the function useful.

An error-detection indicator can now be found on some home players. This is usually a small light that comes on anytime the player detects an error in the data on the disc. While this is a very practical and necessary feature on the professional digital recording decks which inspired it, it is of far less real value for the consumer market. It is interesting primarily as a gauge to indicate

The Pioneer CLD-1010 combination CD player and videodisc player. This type of player handles both CD-Audio discs as well as 8-inch and 12-inch LaserVision videodiscs.

The Technics SL-P520 with frame-accurate cueing. By using the dial on the right side of the front panel, you can precisely begin play at any point on a disc to within ⅟₇₅th-of-a-second accuracy.

exactly how much error correction is required on various discs.

Another feature descended from professional machines is extremely precise cueing of the disc. This feature typically incorporates a dial to enable you to cue the laser pickup to an accuracy of ⅟₇₅th of a second—in essence, *frame-accurate cueing.* This might be useful, for example, in home recording studio applications that require exact manipulation of the audio playback. For the average user, it is probably not worth the extra cost.

PORTABLE PLAYERS

The market for portable CD players has grown so fast that by the beginning of 1987 they were already accounting

SUMMARY OF PLAYER FEATURES

Basic Features

Buttons: Power, Drawer Open/Close, Play, Pause, Fast Forward, Fast Reverse, Skip, Stop

For powering up the player and controlling movement of disc drawer and laser pickup unit. Little significant variation among models.

Auto-Pause

Causes the player to automatically pause at the end of each track; especially useful for listening to one song at a time. Not found on the majority of players.

Track Selection

Buttons used for selecting specific tracks on a disc. Typically involves one or two multipurpose buttons in combination with task-specific buttons. ▶

for more volume sales than any other type of player. The current selection of portables offers features, electronics, and sound quality on a par with most home machines.

Portables come in two varieties: the small *personal* player, and the multi-function *boom box* sound system. It is in the realm of the personal players that size wars are fought. The Sony D-10, for instance, offers a complete system with battery pack that weighs only nine ounces and is no taller than three stacked jewel boxes. The boom boxes, on the other hand, sometimes push the limits of portability.

The successful design of the "Walkman"-type cassette player set portability standards which most CD personal units have followed. They are typically sold with carrying case, headphones, and a rechargeable battery pack that may last for an average of four hours of playing time. The options may include additional battery

Numeric Keypad

For keying track numbers directly rather than pressing the SKIP button numerous times. Found more often on remote control than on the player itself.

Audible Scan

Track remains audible during fast forward or fast reverse. Helpful for locating specific passages. Some models offer two-speed scanning.

Display

Lighted window informs about status of play, number of tracks on disc, and playing time. Wide variety of design.

Convenience Features

Repeat

Allows replay of portions of disc in one or more ways—repeat one track, entire disc, the program, a specified segment of the disc, or random play.

Programmability

Allows for pre-ordering of play sequence. Typically up to 15 tracks, although may range from as few as 8 to as many as 99.

Remote Control

Infrared device allows for operation of player from distances of up to 50 feet. May sometimes be integrated with other components to offer one-point control of VCRs, TVs, cassettes, and receivers as well. ▶

Portable players come in two varieties: the "personal" portable designed for headphone listening, such as the Sony D-10; and the "boom box" portable with built-in radio, cassette deck, and speakers.

packs, often with AC adapters built in, remote control units, auto mounting brackets—the list goes on.

The popularity of the personal portables is enhanced by their ability to play a double role. Many buyers find that plugging a portable into their home component systems works fine, delivering sound and convenience largely equal in quality to home models.

At the other end of the portable spectrum, the boom box systems usually include one or two cassette decks, AM/FM receiver, equalizer, amplifier, and speakers, along with the CD player. Their larger size allows for inclusion of more advanced CD features such as Music Scan, Auto Space, and segment repeat.

Headphone Jack

Either ¼-inch or mini-plug output jack for headphone listening. Some models offer separate volume control for this output.

Special Features

Multiple-Disc Changers

Players which typically hold between 5 and 10 discs, often held in removable cartridges. Some models may hold up to 60 CDs.

▶

AUTO PLAYERS

In addition to the remarkable improvements in tracking stability made to car CD players in recent years, an impressive array of sophisticated features is beginning to appear. Car players now offer most of the basic and many of the standard convenience functions, including 15-track programmability, remotes for track selection and volume, extensive displays, and advanced electronics. The units usually conform to standard dimensions for easy dashboard mounting and often include AM/FM receivers and tone, volume, and balance controls as well.

Many brands offer systems to facilitate loading of discs while driving, a feature usually referred to as *Auto-Load*. Such systems load the CD automatically once the disc is at the entrance of the disc slot. Some auto players incorporate the use of a protective cartridge as well. The

Music Memory

A unique programming feature which allows preprogramming of hundreds of tracks for dozens of individual discs. The machine stores the programs in memory along with a disc recognition code. Player recognizes the disc when reinserted (even after machine is turned off) and calls up your personal program. Offered on only a few machines.

Random Play

A type of programmed playback in which the player itself selects the order of the tracks, mixing them randomly. Called "Shuffle Play" on Sony players.

Auto Scan

Player plays the first few seconds of a track, then moves on to the next. Useful for previewing material on unfamiliar discs.

Random Access by Time within Track

Allows direct minute/second access to any point within a track. Found on only a few players.

Subcode Output

Connection on back of player to output lyrics and graphics stored in the subcode of a disc. Of minimal value—few discs contain subcode graphics, and required display adapter has yet to reach market.

Auto Space (or Auto Silence)

Option found on some machines which causes player to ▶

cartridge is a plastic housing into which the individual discs are preloaded so you never have to handle the disc itself while driving. The cartridges are inserted, just as a cassette might be, with a minimum of attention.

The loading-while-driving issue has been handled ingeniously by Sony in another manner with its CDX-A10 "DiscJockey" model. This two-component system has a small unit containing the controls that mounts on the dashboard. The larger, disc drive/laser unit is installed in the trunk or rear compartment and holds up to 10 discs. You preload the disc magazine, put it in the rear unit, and control play from the dashboard unit.

The CDX-A10 solves two other problems as well: it eliminates disc clutter in the driving area, and it makes the unit more theft-proof. The latter problem has long been a serious concern for car-stereo owners, and with

pause for three to four seconds between tracks. Specifically designed for CD-to-cassette taping.

CD/Cassette-Deck Combination

CD player combined with cassette deck to facilitate the recording of CD material onto tape.

CD/Videodisc Player Combination

A combination player which plays LaserVision videodiscs and audio Compact Discs.

Double-Drawer Player

Player with two disc drawers to allow for continuous programmable play.

Variable Pitch and Tempo Controls

Allow adjustment of pitch and speed to facilitate performing along with the music on the disc. Found on only a few players.

Error-Detection Indicator

A small light that indicates when a data error is detected on the disc.

Frame-Accurate Cueing

Option that allows extremely precise cueing of the disc—typically incorporating a dial to enable positioning of the laser pickup to an accuracy of $1/75$th of a second.

The Sony CDX-A10 DiscJockey™ stores 10 CDs in a changer/player mounted in the trunk of a car. Only the small control unit is located in the passenger compartment.

most car CD players costing in the $600 range, it is a major issue. Other players incorporate standard car-stereo security features such as easy removability or user codes that must be entered before the unit will operate.

PORTABLE CD ON THE ROAD

Deciding between buying a portable player or an auto player can be difficult. You can't take the auto player on a walk or to the beach. And using a portable in the car means either listening with headphones (an unsafe practice which is illegal in some areas) or playing it through battery-powered external speakers.

If your auto already has a tape player, however, a simple $25 solution to the problem is offered by a company called Recoton. The device is marketed as the Compact Disc Adapter and can be used with any already-installed car cassette player.

It consists of a unit which resembles a cassette tape, incorporating a connecting cable with a headphone plug at the end. This goes to the headphone jack of your CD portable, and the unit itself is inserted into the cassette player just like a cassette tape. The stereo signal from the CD player is sent through the cassette heads, into the amplifier, and through the installed stereo speakers in your car. No wiring or permanent installation is required, and no significant signal loss results.

Even if you don't have a cassette player in your car, you still may be able to route sound from your portable CD through your car's speakers. All it takes is an installed FM radio and the "Sound Sender" Mobile Audio Adapter. ▶

The Recoton CD Adapter lets you play the output from a portable player through your car's cassette stereo system.

You plug this unit into your car's 12-volt cigarette lighter socket and attach the mini audio plug to your CD player.

The Sound Sender "broadcasts" the CD audio as an FM signal through your car's wiring system so it can be picked up by your car's FM radio, which you tune to 99.1 MHz. The Sound Sender's audio quality is less than you get with the Recoton unit, but the cost—about $30—clearly beats the price of installing a cassette or CD player in your car. The first models on the market are in mono only, but the manufacturer promises a stereo unit will follow.

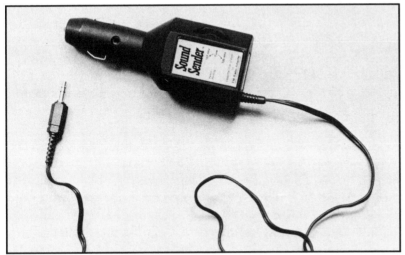

The Sound Sender can play your portable CD player through your car's FM radio system.

CHAPTER 5

CD Hardware Buyer's Guide

So now you're ready. You've seen enough, heard enough, and read enough. You've decided it's time to invest in a CD player. As you should realize after reading the first four chapters, the odds are excellent that you can simply walk into the nearest discount house, pick the first model off the shelf, and get a player that delivers all the sparkle and richness of digital audio. But with a little help and some forethought, you can increase even those odds. By first narrowing your choices to two or three possible machines and taking some time to choose your

dealer, you will almost certainly end up with a machine that meets your expectations, suits your needs, and fits your budget.

WHAT DO YOU WANT?

The three main areas in which you will notice differences among CD players are looks, features, and performance. Each of these affects the price you pay. The cost of circuitry used for extra features and enhanced audio performance adds directly to

a player's price tag. Distinctive styling, too, often commands a higher price, not so much because of the cost of manufacture but because manufacturers understand that sleek design arouses expectations of better quality.

Another factor that affects price is the quality of construction and materials that go into a player. Quality materials generally mean a longer-lasting and more reliable product. The extra cost of a reputable brand-name player may be worth it in the long run.

It should be emphasized, however, that the differences

THREE TYPICAL CD
STARTER SYSTEMS

▼   A typical medium-priced component system would include a home CD player, amplifier, and speakers—all for less than $1000. An FM tuner and cassette deck would round out this home stereo system.

▲   The so-called "rack" or "one-brand" systems, with all components from the same manufacturer and all with the same styling, are typically sold in department stores. A home component system usually offers better value.

◄   You can enjoy top-quality digital audio with nothing more than a portable CD player and a pair of self-powered speakers—usually for no more than $400–$500.

in sound between most models you encounter are likely to be so small as to be almost insignificant to the average listener. Unlike other audio components, there is far less variation in the technical specifications of CD players. To begin the process of narrowing down your choices, you should consider a player's looks, features, and performance, as well as how each affects its price.

Looks

The appearance of the player is an important consideration for many buyers. This is by no means a superficial criterion. While you don't need matching components to achieve high-quality performance from your music system, some attention to aesthetics can add order and symmetry to a listening environment, enhancing the overall experience. After all, it's likely that you'll be spending a lot of time with your player. You should choose one you'll enjoy looking at.

The variety of styles, shapes, and sizes of players on the market make it possible to satisfy just about any taste. While the bulk of players tend to have flat black or brushed metal finishes, you can find a number of variations, including wood-grain and even gold-toned components in a few brands. Some players even may have attachable wood side panels as an accessory.

As more and more players reach the market, you're certain to find greater choice in finishes, styling, and color. The same trend that has enlivened the styling of portable radios and cassettes makes it reasonable to expect a pink CD portable soon. Be aware, however, that if you are committed to having a player with particular features, you may have to settle for standardized appearances.

Another important consideration in getting the right equipment is size. The average home unit weighs about 12 to 15 pounds, while some portables now weigh less than a pound. And while most players seem to be low-profile, slim, and sleek, there is no equating size and shape with quality. The primary consideration in choosing size has to do with where you plan to place the machine. If you already have a mini-component system at home, you may opt to complement it with one of the mini-sized players.

In any case, bear in mind that the appearance of the player should be secondary to its features and performance. And, since most players perform equally well, you will probably spend most of your time looking for the exact combination of features to suit your style of listening.

Features

Remember, certain features are basic to all players while

others are more for the sake of convenience and fun. Of course, the question of price is irrevocably entwined with the array of features on a machine. If you want more sophisticated technology, be prepared to pay extra.

All models—even those costing under $200—should have all the fundamental features in some form or another, providing you with everything you need to play and enjoy discs. Certain low-cost models may even have various mid-priced extras as well, such as extended programmability, or search capabilities. The Scott model DA 952, for example, is a very capable player. Listing for $200, it offers 15-track programmability, full repeat functions, and oversampling digital filters.

Which optional features should you choose in a player? This is a question that only your personal taste can resolve. You should consider convenience features in terms of how and where you plan on listening to CDs.

For example, consumers have grown fond of the remote control unit through its use with TVs and VCRs. You might find this an essential feature for your CD player as well, allowing you to play, pause, select tracks, even set programming from across the room.

A remote control will be essential if you want to control your player from the couch, bed, or jacuzzi. It can be particularly useful if you do a lot of *attentive* listening rather than primarily *background* listening, or if you listen to short-phased music, such as pop or jazz, rather than long-phased music such as classical. In any case, you can expect to pay between $50 and $100 more if you want a remote unit with your player.

The question of how you expect to use your player most—for attentive or background listening—also affects other feature decisions. For example, consider a case of attentive listening. You are a pianist trying to decipher the complexities of a particular performance of a Chopin prelude. Sitting at your piano, you use the remote control to forward and reverse through the piece, locating passages of special interest. You pause the player while you work at the piano to analyze certain sections, resuming play without moving from the keyboard. If you discover particularly difficult segments, you use the A–B repeat function to isolate individual phrases for precise repetition until you are ready to move on.

In another example, imagine that you are relaxing on the couch, listening to an unfamiliar disc. Should you reach a passage that seems too energetic for your meditative mood, you simply auto-scan the disc to hear the first 10 seconds or so of each track. When you find a track that fits your mood, you play it. If it's particularly enjoyable, you can set the player to repeat the track. Use the volume control on the remote to adjust the level, and you can drift off into dreamland.

If you demand even more precise listening, you should consider machines which can cue on index points, or specific time points, within a track. These features, along with Auto Pause and Auto Silence, may also help when copying music to tape.

While some features may be of most use with attentive listening styles, others help most in creating background music environments in the home or in a place of business such as a doctor's office or restaurant. This is especially true of programmable and multidisc units, which allow you to set up hours of uninterrupted, high-quality music. Models with removable cartridges let you store several selected discs in the same cartridge. For example,

you could put a series of New Age or easy-listening discs in one cartridge and country/western in another to create a consistent background sound. Or, using the programming feature, you could play radio DJ, selecting individual tracks from different style discs. And programmable players make it easy for you to select the order of songs for home taping.

Headphone listening is another important consideration. Some people prefer headphones to speakers for the intimate listening environment they offer. They block out ambient room noise, letting you become totally immersed in the sound itself. In addition, they don't disturb others nearby (unless you sing off-key while listening). A headphone jack built into the CD player can be essential if your amplifier doesn't provide one. Be sure to consider whether a separate headphone volume control is also included.

There are numerous other convenience features that have specific appeal to certain buyers. If you are interested in collecting laser videodiscs as well, you would certainly want to look at combination CD/videodisc players. The convenience of one machine that plays all optical disc formats gives these players a definite appeal. On the other hand, it may be more cost-effective to buy two separate units rather than a combination unit.

The question of which convenience features to choose is primarily shaped by personal taste. You set your own criteria. There are other issues, however, that involve more than taste. These have to do with audio design and resulting sound quality—in short, the performance of a player.

Performance

While it is true that differences in performance between CD players are usually small, they do exist. If you are a casual listener, you may find them of little importance. But if you are concerned with the finer points of digital audio reproduction, specific performance criteria can help you decide between players with similar convenience features.

One aspect of player performance that doesn't actually affect the sound quality is the speediness of the player's access time. This specification is usually given in terms of the number of seconds it takes the player to go from one end of a disc to the other. The range of performance is considerable, from as much as six seconds on early models to less than a second on the latest versions. If you're the fast-paced type, quick access time could be important to you.

Overall sound quality is determined by the CD standard itself. But many players go beyond the minimum requirements to enhance the audio by adding digital filtering, oversampling, dual digi-tal-to-analog converters, and additional error-correction circuitry. These enhancements and others, discussed in detail at the end of Chapter 3, in most cases offer improvements in sound quality that are discernible to some people. The best way to determine their effect is not from the salesperson or the brochure, but from sitting down and listening to the players themselves. Comparative listening tests are the only sure method for you to tell if it's worth paying for extra performance features. After all, your ears must be the ultimate judge.

WHICH PLAYER?

When you have considered the range of available options, you should have a good idea of the features that fit your needs. You may even have developed a specific list of the criteria you will use in choosing your player. Now it's time to do a little browsing. In order to make an intelligent buying decision, you will need to narrow your focus to two or three players that meet your basic criteria.

The players are easy to find—they're in almost every hi-fi store, discount chain, and shopping mall throughout the country. Even some record stores and drug stores carry CD players. You should be able to get an ample demonstration of a player's capabilities in any hi-fi showroom, but this doesn't mean you have to buy it there. It's OK to go in and have a look and listen. A good hi-fi store is accustomed to doing a bit of educational work as part of its business. And, while you should keep in mind that listening to any component in a hi-fi showroom means you are experiencing optimal equipment in an optimally designed environment, there still is no better place—short of your own living room—to examine the possibilities. ▶

HOW TO COMPARE THE SOUND OF CD PLAYERS

In response to the standard claims that all CD players sound the same, *Audio Magazine* sponsored a series of scientifically designed and laboratory-controlled listening tests to see if a group of experienced music listeners could detect differences between commercially available players.

The tests were designed by David Clark of DLC Design in Detroit, Michigan. Listeners were asked to switch between three possible sound sources: "A," a reference unit, "B," a "product under test," and a source called "X." The latter was either A or B, randomly chosen by a computer.

The subjects, all members of a Michigan audio club, were to decide whether X was A or B. The tests were "double-blinded," meaning that neither testers nor subjects knew which machine was X in any round of testing.

Volume levels between the machines were exactly matched, and the discs were carefully synchronized so that nothing other than a true sonic difference could alert subjects that a switch to another player had taken place. The subjects were instructed to note only a difference between the sources, not personal preferences.

The players tested ranged from a top-of-the-line $1400 machine to a unit which regularly sells for under $200. The conclusive result was that in two days of continuous testing, none of the 11 subjects could identify machine differences with any consistency—at least, during standard music listening. Certain machines did prove slightly more recognizable when segments from test discs were played. The conductors of the test concluded that, although certain machines may exhibit very subtle sonic "personalities," the differences between properly operating players are so minute as to be almost undetectable.

So what does this mean for the buyer? Is this good news or bad? Since even carefully designed A/B comparison tests can offer little guidance about which players may be the best choice sonically, how can a good choice be made? If you still are plagued by the issue, go do some listening on your own. After all, it's your ears you will be buying for, not those of an anonymous test subject.

Here is a list of suggested listening guidelines when buying any stereo equipment. Applying the same criteria to the CD should help you find one that sounds good to you.

1. Listen for the tonal quality: the high frequencies should be crisp and clear, the mid-range should sound natural, the bass should be full and present. The recording should sound as much as possible like live music.

2. Listen for dimension and position in the stereo image: if you close your eyes, can you visualize a performance area with instruments and voices clearly placed within?

3. Listen to the machine: Is it quiet? Can you hear motor noise during play or the movement of the laser during cueing?

4. Listen for a wide range of dynamics: you should hear the same richness at low volumes as at high volumes, and quiet passages should have the same presence as loud ones.

5. Listen to a variety of discs: test classical, jazz, pop, rock, even spoken-word CDs. Listen to all-digital discs as well as analog recordings. Listen to a test disc with reference tones if one is available.

6. Listen on a variety of systems: try different components and speakers. Most audio store listening rooms can route the player's output through a number of amplifiers, preamplifiers, and speakers. Notice any differences, but remember that each system adds charac-teristic differences of its own.

7. Lastly, try listening with headphones. This is often the purest signal you can get from the player, unaffected by other components.

Don't confuse sonic differences with feature and performance differences. Even though most players sound uniformly good, they may fluctuate widely in their error-correcting abilities or access time.

The good news is that you can shop with the knowledge that whichever player you choose, you will get sound quality more or less consistent with the best on the market. And you can still have the fun of comparing and evaluating to find the player that performs well enough for you to feel that you have scored a terrific deal.

Before you go to the stereo store, prepare yourself by thinking through a few basic questions. For instance:

1. Which players have the specific features I'm interested in?
2. What is the price range of these players?
3. Are there performance differences between these players?

With an idea of what you want in a player, and with a list of questions in mind, you're ready to go out and have some fun. Play with the machines. Test them out. See how they respond and how you feel listening to and using them. These are the most important issues in determining whether you get your money's worth.

In the showroom, you should feel free to examine the prospective players much like you would if buying a car. You shouldn't try to abuse the unit, but do feel free to gently poke, push, and tweak. See how each player feels to the touch. Turn on the power. Try opening and closing the drawer. Call up a few tracks to test the access time. Tap on the display shelf and then the player chassis itself to see if the pick-up mistracks. (Remember, you won't damage the disc or the laser unit by making it skip.) Try performing simple functions such as repeat or programming. The more user-friendly the function, the less time you'll spend at home deciphering instruction manuals. Finally, stop the disc and gently heft the player to see if it feels sturdy and well-built.

If you're determined to make the most accurate comparisons possible, feel free to take along a disc or two to play. Include at least one high-quality digitally recorded disc of music you like, especially one you may have heard before. Various manufacturers also offer special discs to test for technical specifications of a player.

Asking questions of salespeople gives you two kinds of information. First, you get details about specific players and options, helping you build a supply of knowledge on which to base your final decision. Second, you also get a feel for the general competency and helpfulness of the people representing each dealer. If you buy from a hi-fi dealer, it's important to find one you feel comfortable with. There is a wide range of competence among stereo salespeople, and you are strongly advised to take time to find those you can trust. Personal recommendations from friends or business associates can help you find reputable firms.

At this stage in your shopping, you may also want to get additional opinions about specific CD models. You can find useful sources of information at your local newsstand to help you evaluate the players. There are any number of dependable audio publications that regularly publish reviews of the latest crop of players. (Most of these publications, many of which are listed in Chapter 8, also publish reviews of discs.) If you feel a need to delve more deeply into the actual workings of digital audio than we are doing here, consult one or more of the books we recommend for additional information on digital technology and storage (see Suggestions for Further Reading and Listening).

Perhaps the best method for evaluating players is to talk to other people. If you have friends who own players, visit them and spend some time in a relaxed setting getting the feel of one player. Nothing beats hands-on experience, and the impressions of a CD owner can offer practical insights.

After you have completed enough research to satisfy your concerns, choose two or three specific models that seem right for your needs. If you haven't narrowed your choices down that far, then you may still not be ready to make a purchase. When you go to the store to make your final decision, know the exact brands and model numbers, list prices, and features the players offer.

WHERE TO BUY

There are three primary sources for buying a CD player: hi-fi specialty stores, discount houses, and mail-order firms. Where can you get the best deal? When even your local department store carries brand-name players at seemingly terrific prices, why should you go to a hi-fi specialty store that offers limited discounts?

Indeed, the differences in price between dealers can be startling. The manufacturer's list price is only a point of reference. As an example, consider a player such as the Sony CDP-310, with programmability, remote control, and digital filtering. The manufacturer's list price is $399. Yet a quality hi-fi shop may have it on its shelves for $349, and during a sale the price may go as low as $299. A nearby discount chain sells the same player for a flat $299. And a Chicago-based mail-order house offers it at $249.95, a considerable savings over list price.

But price is not the only consideration. There is usually a correlation between price and service. Before you choose, it is a good idea to evaluate the various dealerships on a few basic points:

1. Will I get what I order?
2. Are there hidden charges (shipping and handling, credit card surcharges, etc.) in buying from a mail-order firm?

3. How do I feel about the trustworthiness of this dealer? Do I feel comfortable talking with the salespeople?

4. And most important: What kind of follow-up or support can I expect (return policies, on-site repair, etc.)?

Once you have decided on the player you want and the dealer you wish to buy it from, you are ready to make your purchase. If you have chosen a mail-order house or a discount chain, there is usually not a great deal more to do than place a phone call or plunk down the money.

If however, you have chosen a hi-fi dealer, you may have the option of trying to negotiate the best deal. In almost every case, the price you see marked on the player in the store, even if it is below list price, is not the lowest price the dealer can sell it for and still make a profit. In other words, you still have bargaining room if you want it.

To begin with, if you have carefully done your research, you may know that the same player is sold for less at another store down the street. Make this known to the dealer, emphasizing that you are definitely going to buy the model and would rather buy from this store—perhaps just because you like the way it does business. You may find that the dealer will opt to sell you the player for the competitive price rather than let you take your cash elsewhere. After all, even one-fourth of the sales commission may be better than no commission at all. So don't automatically assume that the first quoted price is unnegotiable.

If you are considering additional stereo purchases, you may have another bargaining chip. Explain to the salesperson that you are also in the market for a new set of speakers and if the price is right, you might be willing to buy everything at once. Often this is just the incentive a dealer needs to offer you a package price. It is thoroughly possible that with some shrewd negotiating you can find all the components you want at a reliable local dealer, and at prices very near what you might have paid an impersonal mail-order house.

And don't forget the question of service after the sale. If you are an average audio user, you may prefer to have a good working relationship with a dealer who will personally take charge of repairs or ship-backs. You may even be able to arrange for "service loaners" to replace equipment that will be gone for more than a couple of weeks.

On the other hand, if you are a competent tinkerer, with lots of experience working with advanced electronics, you may not need any added care for your equipment. In that case you may feel comfortable choosing the no-nonsense, bottom-line deals that can be found through a mail-order firm.

BRING IT HOME AND PLUG IT IN

When you finally get your new CD player home, hooking it up to your stereo system is very easy. It requires no special tools or skills. First choose a space for the player within the arrangement of your stereo system, preferably not more than three feet from the amplifier or preamplifier. The design of your player will suggest the most convenient location. If you should have a top-loading model, you will of course need adequate room above the unit. But since the vast majority of players load by means of a slide-out tray on the front panel, you can probably place it between other components.

Before you position the player, read the owner's manual carefully to get to know the particulars of your model. For example, check to see whether the unit has a *laser pickup lock-down mecha-*

PROFILE OF A HI-FI DEALER

How do you find a good hi-fi dealer? One way is to turn to *AudioVideo International* magazine's prestigious Retailer of the Year Awards. There, for instance, you would find Magnolia Hi-Fi and Video, of Seattle, Washington. Selected as one of the top three 1986 retailers in the country by electronics manufacturers, suppliers, and representatives, Magnolia has won the top honors in 8 of the last 10 years since the awards were first given.

A visit to any of Magnolia's seven stores will give you an idea of what a specialty hi-fi dealer can offer. Magnolia carries CD players from many major brands, including mid-priced models from Denon, Sony, Pioneer, and Technics, and high-end players from McIntosh, Carver, Nakamichi, and Tandberg.

A good specialty store attracts customers by offering excellent service. Magnolia has a full-time service department equipped to adjust and repair almost all of the audio, video, and mobile electronics equipment the company sells. This pays off for the customer in two ways. The first concerns timely repairs. You don't usually have to wait several weeks while your broken CD player is sent to a factory across the country. And second, the store's technicians quickly get to know which CD players are built to last. As a result, only players with a good reputation for reliability continue to appear on the store shelves.

Dave Kaplan, Magnolia's audio buyer, stresses the importance of buying from a well-established store that services what it sells. That, along with an extended warranty contract, is the best way to protect your investment. Kaplan also suggests you find a salesperson you feel comfortable with. ▶

nism. Most models have some means for securing the pickup during shipment so it doesn't bounce around. You will need to unlock this before using the player. You usually do so by moving a sliding switch or loosening a set screw.

If you have a remote control, make sure that you have a clear vantage of the machine when you point the device from your preferred listening area. Since most remotes use a beam of infrared light to send control signals, they require a direct, unobstructed path to the front panel of the player. Consider also where you prefer to store the discs themselves. While most can be stored out of the way, you may want to allow for a little extra room near the player to keep your current favorites.

After you have familiarized yourself with the manual and positioned your player, you only need to attach the connection cable. These invariably are supplied with the unit

"Don't be afraid to ask how long the salesperson has been there," he advises. "And don't let yourself be pressured. A good salesperson does not have to hard-sell you."

Another indicator of a good store is fair policies on returns, exchanges, and warranties. Get a written copy of the policies and examine the terms carefully. Magnolia offers a full refund within 7 days or exchange privileges within 30 days. However, if a store's policies seem *too* good, you may pay for it in higher prices.

and have left and right RCA connectors at either end. Connect the pair at one end to the right/left output jacks on the rear of your player and the pair at the other end

Magnolia Hi-Fi and Video's CD showroom for medium-priced component players.

to a corresponding set of right/left input jacks on the

Magnolia Hi-Fi and Video's showroom for high-end CD systems. Included are CD players from Carver, Tandberg, McIntosh, and Nakamichi.

rear of your preamplifier, amplifier, or receiver. In most cases, the input jacks will be labeled AUX, CD AUX, or TAPE MONITOR. Do not plug them into the PHONO jack, because the line voltage will be mismatched. Refer to the owner's manuals of both your player and stereo system for specific set-up information regarding your particular equipment.

Now you only need to plug the power cord into the nearest AC (a grounded, po-

larized outlet is preferred) and activate the power switch. Press the button to open the drawer, drop in a disc, and press PLAY. Adjust the volume by using the master controls of your system. If you don't hear sound, check to see that you have selected the correct input jack (AUX, CD AUX, or TAPE MONITOR). With the player correctly installed, your stereo system should issue forth the best sounds it has ever produced.

Once you've had a chance

to experiment with the features and listen to the sound, ask yourself: "Do I like what I got?" If you have carefully followed the steps outlined above, taking advantage of all the information available to you, chances are you will experience 100 percent satisfaction. If not, don't be afraid to say so. Immediately take the player back and try to arrange for an adjustment. Most reputable dealers (and even many discount houses and department stores) have an interest in creating satisfied customers. If you take the equipment back in undamaged condition, with all the original packing and instructions, chances are you will be able to at least trade for a machine more to your liking. Even if a mail-order house refuses to return or exchange equipment purchased from it, all is not lost. You should be able to sell the player through the classified ads for what you paid for it. After all, the mail-order price was probably at least 25 percent below list price.

Once you have a player you're satisfied with, you can expect years of trouble-free operation—with nothing to maintain. There is nothing to clean, adjust, or replace on a normally functioning CD player.

UPGRADING YOUR SOUND SYSTEM FOR DIGITAL AUDIO

Along with the flood of new CD players and signal processing equipment, there have been a number of other audio components (such as amplifiers, speakers, and headphones) promoted as "digital-ready," and "digital-compatible." Such claims can

CD-PLAYER MAINTENANCE

Why Nothing Is Required

The Compact Disc player is virtually maintenance-free, unlike a phonograph turntable, which requires extensive cleaning and the use of dust covers to provide a clean environment for the records. Any accumulation of dust or lint in the phonograph playing area results in rapid buildup of noise and distortion. It is not uncommon to find minute clumps of debris clinging to the needle after playing a single LP.

The CD player, by contrast, is well sealed, so that dust rarely enters the chassis. There is no contact between the pickup and the disc to cause buildup of debris. Dust on

a disc can be easily cleaned off. Furthermore, any dust on the surface of the disc that could obscure access to data is usually compensated for by the error-correction system.

Turntables require careful set-up and adjustment, and the phono cartridges—which cost between $25 and $250 to replace—start wearing out the minute they begin playing a record. Nothing of the sort is necessary with the CD player. It works fine on any level surface. And since the laser pickup is factory-set, it should never be tampered with by the consumer. And if it ever needs replacement, this should be done by a trained technician.

Even tape players require occasional maintenance procedures. At the very least, the heads and rollers must be cleaned periodically to prevent diminished sound quality. Cleaning requires the purchase of various cleaning cassettes, solutions, and brushes. In addition, the large number of moving mechanical parts tends to cause problems. If you have ever had a tape player "eat" a cassette, you know that the resulting mangle of tape can mean not only the loss of a favorite cassette, but quite possibly a repair bill for the cassette player.

Of course, no electronic equipment is beyond the occasional malfunction. If you should have a serious problem with the unit, don't try to repair it yourself unless you have considerable experience with electronics. Practically every component of a CD player is sealed away and requires specialized tools and instruments to properly repair. The laser, for instance, is carefully sealed in its housing so that it poses no threat to the user. Refer any problems to the dealer from which your player was purchased or to a competent hi-fi repair shop.

Some dealers offer extended service contracts which you may purchase. A three-year contract may cost less than $100. Essentially, it's an insurance policy against repair costs. The higher the value of your investment, the more sense this coverage makes. When considering a service contract, look for the actual benefits it offers—does it cover parts cost, labor, shipping? Are there exclusions which might make it of less value to you?

Watch out for deals that sound too good to be true. The prospect of collecting money for future services often proves tempting for unscrupulous operators. Get your service contract from a *reputable* dealer.

You should, of course, observe the standard care procedures required by any piece of stereo gear. The player, for example, should not be placed next to an extreme heat source or exposed to dampness or high humidity. The power cord should not be pinched or clamped by other equipment, and the unit should not be placed on a surface prone to heavy vibrations or jolting movement. With sensible treatment and care, you should get years of top-quality performance out of your player with a minimum of maintenance.

be confusing to the consumer who may hesitate to buy a CD player for fear of needing to replace all or part of an existing system. In truth, these labels are mostly "hype." Almost any mid-priced stereo system should be quite capable of handling a CD player.

Still, any audio component performs best when linked to comparable equipment. A stereo system is only as strong as its weakest component. If there are components in your current system with which you are unhappy, chances are their shortcomings will only become more annoying with the addition of a CD player. Here are some tips on what to look for in an audio component in order to get maximum performance from your CD player.

Amplifiers

Your current amplifier may well be adequate for playback of LPs and cassettes. To compensate for limited dynamic range, the sound on most analog playback media is *compressed* during the recording process: loud signal peaks are squelched and soft passages are boosted. In this way, softer sections can be played loud enough to mask the background noise of the system without louder passages becoming unpleasantly loud.

Because of the CD's naturally large dynamic range, very little is done in the way of compression of its signal. This means the natural dynamics of the performance are better represented, with little or no artificial manipulation of the signal. Since your tendency may be to boost the system volume to take advantage of this distortion-free range, your amplifier must be capable of handling short bursts of peak signal.

Keep in mind that the advantage of a more powerful amplifier is not simply to let you play the system louder. The high peak levels common to uncompressed CD sound require the amplifier to deliver occasional, split-second increases to 100 watts or more. An amplifier with plenty of peak power, or *dynamic headroom*, can deliver these bursts without distorting. Less powerful amplifiers may not be damaged by these peaks but they will not be capable of delivering the clean, undistorted sound you expect from the CD.

Although most amplifiers are perfectly capable of delivering clean sound from a CD player, it is preferable to have extra power if you want to play CD music louder. Unless you have a low-cost system rated in its technical specifications at less than 25 watts per channel, you should have no problems.

Speakers

Along with an increase in amplifier power comes the need for speakers capable of accommodating the added signal load. It is probably a helpful rule of thumb to say that if you can afford to upgrade only one area of your system, your speakers should get first attention. While an underpowered amplifier can function quite acceptably with higher rated speakers, the inverse is not true. Speakers that are underrated for a powerful amplifier will commonly distort at the higher sound-pressure levels and quickly detract from your listening experience.

Speaker cabinet design can be important as well, and involves more than appearance. The physical construction of the housing should be able to withstand the increased vibrations at higher volume levels often incurred with CD players. A higher price tag does not necessarily mean that the speakers are better built for loud sounds. Examine the construction for yourself, and don't be afraid to turn up the volume when you're testing speakers in the stereo showroom.

It is essential that speakers be able to handle the power ratings of your amplifier. Speakers functioning just below their upper limits on a phonograph-based system may be pushed beyond those limits by the uncompressed peak levels and deeper bass delivered by a well-produced CD. The result will be distortion at higher volume levels. Typically, a speaker will be rated for minimum and maximum power capabilities. If you read that a speaker is recommended for use with amplifiers delivering up to 200 watts, you can feel pretty certain that a CD played through a 200-watt amplifier will not be able to damage it.

Often speakers are rated in terms of sensitivity, or the ability to deliver a maximum *sound pressure level* (SPL). In general, the higher the better. If one pair of speakers is rated at 80 dB SPL and another at 100 dB, the second pair is less likely to overload during the high peak levels. Sensitivity ratings can usually help you draw accurate conclusions about the proper components. Technical reviews found in audio magazines and guides are excellent references for gathering further information and opinions.

Just remember that even the best-looking speaker or the one with the best technical specifications is not right for you if you don't like its sound. Regardless of whether a CD player is involved, the best way to choose speakers is to find those that sound good to you. There are subtle differences in the quality of sound among various speakers, regardless of the price range. A good stereo showroom will be equipped to let you audition a variety of speakers using the same sound source. Trust your ears, then choose the best-sounding ones you can afford.

Headphones

Headphones are becoming ever more popular as a means to private, unintrusive listening enjoyment. Their popularity in recent years clearly has been boosted by Walkman-type personal stereos. But the cheap, compact headphones which accompany such units are often inadequate to handle the wallop packed by the CD. The array of new headphones specifically designed to meet digital demands perhaps most deserves the "digital-ready" slogans.

To begin with, the superlight, open-air headphones of the last 10 years are giving way to models which seal off the space around the ear. Unlike the awkward, bulky "cans" of decades past, the new models use lightweight foam and plastic to combine the comfort of open-air with the enclosed-ear design ideal for capturing the full range of CD frequency response. And lightweight but powerful magnets deliver full-powered sound. While some models seem to offer unnecessary range—from 15 Hz to 30 kHz, for example—the extra capability may insure an even and smooth performance within the audible range.

Shop by listening to various models, playing the same disc on one player. Look for those offering higher *sensitivity*, measured in milliwatts (mW). Most quality headphones should be rated at least at 105 dB/mW. Also consider the *impedance*, rated in ohms (Ω). The impedance should match that of your player's headphone output. Check the published specifications for each product. The higher the impedance, the less power required to attain the same signal level.

Check also for durability. Headphones receive considerable stress even from ordinary use. Make sure the *armature*—the curved band connecting the left and right sides—is well constructed and easily adjusted. The cables themselves receive constant abuse from tension and sudden tugs. Make sure they are sturdy and well attached.

The headphone's plug (and the jack on the player in which you insert it) comes in two common sizes: the standard ¼-inch diameter plug and the smaller mini-plug often found on personal stereos. It's not a serious problem if the jack on your player is a different size from the plug on your headphones. You can purchase a simple adapter for either size at most consumer electronics stores.

Plan on spending between $30 and $100 for a satisfactory pair of headphones. The lower-priced models may be perfectly adequate, but the upper-end models will likely provide more of the punch and dynamic response you'll want from the CD. Most importantly, make sure they fit comfortably. Your ears are unique and what may be preferable for someone else might not work for you.

Extras

You will discover a wide range of extras and accessories designed for CD systems—everything from do-it-yourself acoustical paneling modules for designing your home listening space, to vibration-dampening base plates to provide a more stable foundation for your player.

Just remember, you don't need any of this to enjoy good digital audio on your home system. You can play and enjoy your CD player on practically any equipment—even headphones alone. But, you will clearly benefit from the best equipment you can afford. The precision, crisp-ness, and clarity of CD sound should be given the best possible path to your ears. Depending on how avidly you pursue your hobbies, all these products can contribute to the building of the perfect system. Be prudent, but have fun.

PART THREE

The
Disc

CHAPTER 6

It's in the Pits:
How CDs Are Made

It's interesting to note that Edison's metallic cylinders, which began the tradition of prerecorded music in the home over one hundred years ago, and the silvery Compact Discs, which now introduce the next phase of it, utilize essentially the same concept—indentations in a metallic surface.

Seen under a microscope, these distant cousins might look like landscapes of two distinct alien worlds. The former, with large chasms like the Grand Canyon. The latter, more like a futuristic city, lined with symmetrical boulevards and flow paths.

Edison's foil-covered wax cylinder and the Philips/Sony Compact Disc both grew from the same inspired vision: that the vibrational character of sound can be physically recorded and reproduced. The integrity of the reproduced sound increases as more detail and accuracy are achieved in each stage of the process.

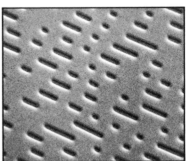

Microphotographs of a record groove and the pits on a CD. The distance between the two peaks of the record groove is about 90 μm. The distance between two adjacent tracks of pits is 1.6 μm.

Of course, the most significant difference between the Compact Disc and its predecessors—cylinders, records, and tapes—is the basic method of encoding the sound. The CD has brought consumer audio out of the analog realm and into the digital age. It's literally music-by-numbers.

How are these numbers used to make it sound as if Lionel Richie, Luciano Pavarotti, or the London Symphony Orchestra is performing in your living room? It is not quite as mysterious as it may seem. Let's begin with the structure of the disc itself.

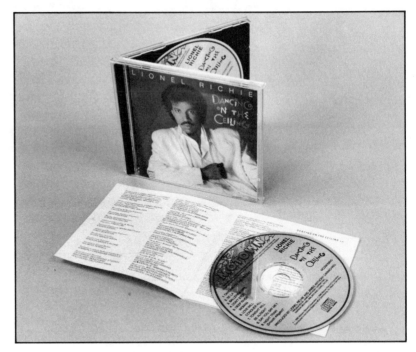

The Compact Disc and its jewel-box package. The CD is rapidly growing in popularity as a high-quality music medium.

DISC STRUCTURE

The Compact Disc has a diameter of 120 mm, or about 4 ¾ inches. It is 1.2-mm thick (about ¹⁄₂₀th of an inch) and weighs about 14 grams, or ½ ounce. A 15-mm diameter hole in the center is used for positioning the disc on the drive shaft. The silvery, prismatic underside is the surface which the laser reads, and the top is imprinted with the label information.

The disc is constructed of three components:

1. The base, or substrate, of the disc, usually made from optical-grade polycarbonate plastic, an extremely hard type of Plexiglass.

2. A very thin reflective coating, usually of aluminum or silver.

3. A protective acrylic resin sealing layer that forms the top of the disc, on the surface of which the disc label is silk-screened.

It is into the plastic substrate base that the pits are molded during the manufacturing process. The thin metal coating serves as a mirrored surface that reflects the laser beam after it passes through the molded substrate. The protective layer seals the digital data encoded in the pits from the ravages of everyday use.

Most of the area on the disc is available for storing data. The major exception is the clamping area, a 16-mm-wide band surrounding the center hole. This is the portion of the disc that is physically clamped down by a mechanism in the CD player in order to hold it firmly while spinning the disc.

The area of the disc which holds the data is partitioned into three sections:

1. The lead-in segment

The Compact Disc is manufactured to very precise tolerances, a fact which helps ensure that any disc can play in any player.

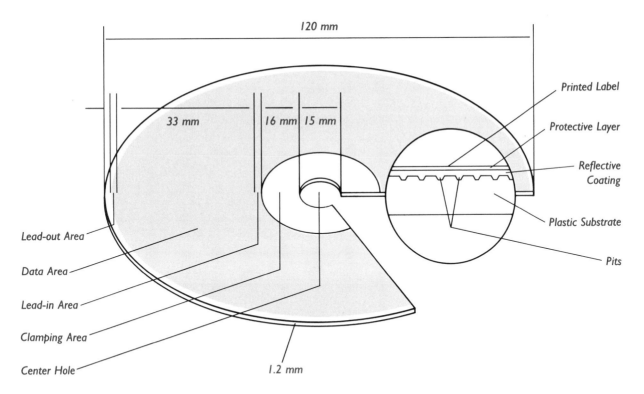

It's in the Pits: How CD's Are Made • 91

(2-mm wide), which holds digital operational data, including a "table of contents," for the entire disc.

2. The program area (up to 33-mm wide), which can store up to two billion pits in about twenty thousand revolutions of the spiral track.

3. The lead-out portion (1-mm wide), which signals the end of the disc.

Unlike a conventional record player, a CD player begins reading the program on a Compact Disc at the inner edge of the data area and continues outward until it reaches the lead-out area.

The overall dimensions of a disc are expressed above in millimeters, or mm. The millimeter—which is equivalent to about $\frac{1}{25}$th of an inch—is a convenient measure for this purpose. However, when we delve into the microscopic world of the pits on a CD, we need a smaller unit: the micrometer (μm).

The micrometer is $\frac{1}{1000}$th of a millimeter, or about $\frac{1}{25,000}$th of an inch.

The data tracks are made up of alternating pits and lands, the flat areas between the pits. The successive loops of the track formed by the pits and lands are approximately 1.6 micrometers apart and spiral outward from the center of the disc. So densely packed are they that a human hair laid down in parallel with them would cover about 60 adjacent tracks.

When you pick up a CD and view it in normal light, you'll see a rainbow of colors on its silvery surface. The colors are not imbedded in the disc or printed on its exterior. They are beams of normal white light that are *diffracted* by the pattern of tracks on the disc. Because the distance between adjacent tracks is so small, each successive loop of the track acts as a tiny prism, reflecting and scattering the different wavelengths, i.e., different colors,

of white light to create the rainbow effect.

The length of each pit and land varies according to the data encoded there. A pit or land may measure from about 0.8 to 3 micrometers in length. To maintain the proper spacing between adjacent loops of the spiral track, each pit must be very close to 0.5 micrometers wide. And the depth of each pit, about 0.1 micrometer, is critical for proper reflection of the laser light.

DATA STRUCTURE

Since digital numbers are made up of ones and zeroes, you might expect that each pit on a CD would represent a one, and each land a zero in the original data stream. However, if an approach like that were used, a CD would store less than an hour of sound, and would not operate as reliably as it does. Instead, a one is represented

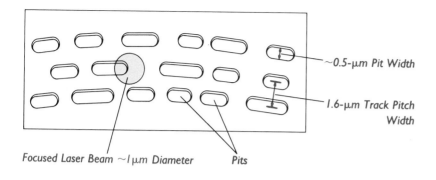

~0.5-μm Pit Width

1.6-μm Track Pitch Width

Focused Laser Beam ~1 μm Diameter   Pits

The pits on a CD are the smallest mass-produced formations manufactured today. A human hair would cover up about sixty turns of the spiral track.

when the track changes from a pit to a land or from a land to a pit. The variable distance between the pit/land transitions represents from 2 to 10 zeroes, with the distance corresponding to the number of zeroes.

Each digit (zero or one) occupies about 0.278 micrometers along the track. For example, the shortest allowable pit (or land) represents three digits—two zeroes and a one—and is 0.834 micrometers long (three times 0.278). The longest pit (or land) represents 11 digits—10 zeroes and a one—and is about 3.058 micrometers long.

This method of encoding

requires a data stream that has many more zeroes than ones. But the original data stream of the digital audio samples has a more or less even distribution of zeroes and ones. That is why the final step of processing the data before encoding them on the disc is the modulation process called *EFM*, or eight-to-fourteen modulation. It translates every 8 bits of the audio data into 14 bits of data containing more zeroes, thus creating a modulated data stream suitable for storage as pits and lands on the disc. (See the box below on CIRC and EFM for a description of how EFM works.)

Whereas the length of the pits and lands contains the modulated data stream, the depth of the pits is important for proper reading of the data. The depth of each pit— about 0.1 micrometer (or 110 *nanometers*)—is very close to ¼ of the wavelength of the refracted light from the laser. This property of the pits results in *phase cancellation* of the reflected light as described in Chapter 3, allowing the photodetector to translate the flickering of the light into a digital bit stream represented by the pits and the lands.

The designers of the Compact Disc use the bit stream to carry more than the audio data. During the recording and manufacturing processes it is supplemented with additional data bits that help the player synchronize the decoding of the data and correct data errors resulting from scratches and dirt on the disc's surface.

The synchronization and error-correction data are essential to the proper demodulation of the data during playback. But additional data are needed to help the CD player find its way around the disc. If you press a button to go to track 7, the player needs a way to find that track on the disc. Also, the player needs information on the elapsed and remaining playing time for the display.

This information about disc tracks and timing is carried in the *subcode*. Subcode data appear in two places on the disc: first, in the table of contents in the lead-in area at the beginning of the disc. The table of contents tells the player how many tracks are on the disc as well as the playing time for each track and for the entire disc. You'll often see the total number of tracks and playing time dis-

CIRC and EFM

Two technical acronyms that you may hear bandied about by CD aficionados are *CIRC* and *EFM*. CIRC stands for Cross Interleaved Reed–Solomon Code. It was developed at MIT by Irving S. Reed and Gustave Solomon as a method of digital data error correction long before the advent of the CD. As used on the CD, CIRC accomplishes two things: it generates error-correction codes (check codes and parity bits) that can be used to detect and correct errors due to defects on the disc; and it spreads out, or interleaves, segments of disc data so that if one portion of a frame is not readable, the other portions—which are physically located at different points on the disc—can be used to calculate the lost data and correct the errors.

The inclusion of CIRC error codes increases the amount of data stored by about a third. But their use is essential for high-quality audio. Without CIRC, the audio data would have about one erroneous bit for every 100,000 bits. That may not sound like much, but it would be enough to cause lots of audible clicks and tracking glitches during the playback of a CD. After CIRC codes are added, the bit error rate for a CD drops to less than one bad bit in 10 million, a level that results in almost perfect sound from the Compact Disc.

EFM stands for eight-to-fourteen modulation, the method of converting the digital audio values to specific patterns of zeroes and ones that define the length of the pits and lands on the disc. Eight-to-fourteen modulation is the last processing of the data before they are encoded on the disc. Each of the 16-bit audio samples is divided to produce two 8-bit data values. The EFM process then translates each 8-bit data value into a corresponding 14-bit value so that at least two zeroes separate each one, as the following excerpt from an EFM translation table illustrates:

8-bit data values	14-bit EFM patterns
01100100	01000100100010
01100101	00000000100010
01100110	01000000100100
01100111	00100100100010
01101000	01001001000010
01101001	10000001000010
01101010	10010001000010

The 14-bit patterns are the actual strings of zeroes and ones that are stored on the disc. The scheme of representing zeroes as the distance between pit/land transitions requires that at least two zeroes separate each one in the stored data stream. That is why the 8-bit values, many of which do not meet this requirement, must be translated into longer 14-bit values which do have enough separating zeroes. Also, 3 *merging bits* are added to each 14-bit pattern as separators. The result is that for each 8 bits of original audio data, 17 bits are stored on the discs.

During playback, the data decoding system first strips off the 3 merging bits and then demodulates the data, translating the 14-bit patterns back into their corresponding 8-bit data values. These values are recombined into the original audio data stream for conversion to sound output from the player.

played on the front panel when a disc is first inserted. The player's control system also uses the data from the table of contents to prevent you from accessing or programming a track that doesn't exist on a disc.

Second, subcode data are stored throughout the tracks on the disc, interwoven with the audio data. These data tell the player where it is on the disc, and provide the track and timing information for access and display.

A Compact Disc may have from 1 to 99 tracks. The length of a track is measured in minutes and seconds of playing time, and is limited only by the storage space on the disc. Each second of playing time is further subdivided into 75 *frames*. The frame is the smallest unit of sound on the disc that the player can access. Each frame contains the audio data for $1/75$th of a second of stereo sound. In addition to information about the track number, minute, second, and frame number, the subcode interwoven in the audio also contains data numbering the index points within a track. Index points, a further subdivision sometimes used for long tracks, are explained in Chapter 4.

DISC MANUFACTURING

The immense amount of precisely positioned data on a Compact Disc (some fifteen billion bits in all) and the microscopic size of the pits (the smallest manufactured formation in any industry) presented unprecedented challenges to the engineers who designed the disc manufacturing process. In most cases, they had to design and build the very machines they were incorporating into their speculative production process.

As a result, during the first few years of the CD's exposure to the international market, there were hardly

---

SUBCODE GRAPHICS: TV PICTURES FROM A COMPACT DISC

In addition to containing a disc's track and timing information, other portions of the subcode are available for the disc producer to store whatever data might be desired. This extra storage space on the disc was originally intended to carry still pictures or text of the lyrics that could be displayed on a television screen in synchrony with the music. But this arrangement requires an extra connector on the player and another piece of hardware to decode the subcode and display it on the TV.

In 1985, the first CD with subcode graphics was released. It was the Firesign Theatre's *Eat or Be Eaten*, an audio comedy about playing an interactive CD game. The disc contains about a hundred pictures encoded in the subcode channels.

The TV pictures from subcode graphics, however, proved too static and cartoon-like to warrant further development for the consumer market. Although many players have been produced with subcode output jacks on the rear panel, no decoding hardware to support subcode graphics has appeared on the market. The pictures on *Eat or Be Eaten* lie dormant in the pits of the disc, bypassed by a rapidly advancing technology that promises to supply high-quality images from the CD-Video and CD-Interactive formats described in Chapter 10.

---

enough manufacturing plants to keep up with the demand. Until 1985, the bulk of all CDs was produced in either Germany or Japan at plants owned by PolyGram, Sony, and JVC. The prohibitive costs (upwards of $30 million) and first-generation riskiness of building a CD plant kept the initial participants few in number. Since 1985 and the start of the CD's popular success, however, new plants are appearing with regularity. More than 15 plants are scheduled to be on-line in the U.S. alone by the end of 1987.

This increase in manufacturing capacity will prove to be a factor in the potential drop in CD prices and the availability of more of all kinds of discs. As the major labels become convinced of the CD's longevity, they, as well as numerous independent companies, will make an investment in the future of the Compact Disc.

One factor in the cost of manufacturing CDs is the need for extremely clean conditions. Unlike phonograph pressing operations, which are primarily mechanical operations, many parts of a CD production facility must be kept virtually dirt and dust free. Since a pit is only $\frac{1}{120}$th the size of an average dust particle, one single bit of

dust can easily render a disc unusable. Furthermore, the operation of high-tech equipment such as the injection-molding presses which fashion the discs demands stringent clean-room conditions.

The workers in a CD plant manufacturing area wear protective clothing and face masks. Anyone or anything entering the clean area must go through air showers to remove all particles of contaminants. Raw materials coming in from outside are carefully treated and isolated to ensure that no contaminants enter with them. The halls and meeting rooms of even the public areas are typically spotless, and visitors can glimpse the workings of the plant itself only through airtight glass windows.

The requirements for clean rooms and precision manufacturing directly affect the quality and productivity of the manufacturing operation. Such concerns contributed to the difficulties of getting plants running and producing

fast enough to meet consumer demand.

The process itself does bear certain resemblances to the LP pressing process, in the sense that discs are pressed from a metal mold. But CD manufacturing is essentially very different than pressing LPs. The initial form used in CD manufacture, the *master*, is made from a *premaster* ¾-inch video tape that contains the digital audio data. Technicians use the master disc to create a negative image on a metal plate called a "father." The father is then used to create a series of "mothers," which are again the positive image. From the mothers, a series of "sons" are made which serve as the molds in the injection-molding machines. In these machines, the plastic substrate is forced under high pressure into the mold which imprints it with the audio information.

Mastering

The master itself is typically made on discs of specially prepared glass called *float glass*. These glass masters are about 220 mm in diameter and 6 mm thick. The float glass is made by pouring molten glass onto a molten metal such as tin. The plates of glass are then chemically treated and polished to create a perfectly flat, smooth surface.

These plates are tested for uniformity by a laser and, if acceptable, are coated with a layer of *photoresist* material into which the pits are burned by another laser. The thickness of this photoresist surface is carefully monitored by laser to precisely accommodate the pit depth. The coated plate is then heat-cured and stored for use. The glass master can be recycled after use.

Like the construction of the glass master, the actual burning of the spiral track into the photoresist surface of the master is done under the strictest clean-room standards. The mastering laser is part of an ultraprecise high-tech machine which is fully automated and closed off inside its own clean room. It rarely comes in contact with humans or the outside world.

The glass disc is placed on the cutting lathe with its photoresist layer exposed to the beam of the main cutting laser—one more powerful than the laser in a CD player. The main laser is guided by a smaller laser which focuses and tracks the cutting laser in much the same way the laser pickup in your player reads a disc. As the disc rotates at speeds from 200 to 500 rpm, an opto-acoustic shutter, driven by the digital premaster tape, turns the mastering laser on and off, burning the pits into the surface of the photoresist material as the tape plays.

After the glass master has had the tracks burned in by the main laser, the disc then moves to an automatic developer machine. Here it is washed in developing fluid until the burned-in portions

Cross-sectional views of steps in the CD-manufacturing process, from glass master to finished disc.

have been etched to the proper pit depth.

Injection Molding

Next the master disc is taken to an electroplating room where a silver-plating process yields a negative image of the tracks and pits of the master. This father is then used to generate the series of mothers and sons which are used as the stampers in the injection mold.

The finished stampers are mounted in the injection molds for the infusion of the polycarbonate plastic which will make up the bulk of the finished CD. Getting the polycarbonate into the mold is a rather involved process in itself. The raw plastic material is shipped in tiny-pellet form. This must be transferred to the pressing area without taking any dust or contaminant from the outside world with it.

The pellets are drawn by vacuum into a drying area where any moisture is re-moved. Moisture would result in bubbles or blemishes in the substrate. A mechanical conveyor moves the pellets from the dryer into a hopper where they are melted just prior to being injected in measured amounts into the mold. The plastic is forced into the mold and the two halves of the mold separate to dislodge the imprinted substrate. The entire process takes about 15 seconds.

The discs are immediately scanned for flaws by another laser. Dust flecks, water bubbles, and other contaminants show up as black spots. Warpage and malformation are also revealed in this process and any defective discs are discarded.

Additional Layering

Next, the substrates embedded with the pits are moved to a room where they receive the reflective coating. This process may take place in either of two ways. In the vacuum-deposition method,

A glass master disc. The pits on the master disc provide the pattern for all subsequent molding steps.

an aluminum "fog" is created by vaporizing ingots of the metal in a vacuum chamber which holds the substrates. The resulting metallic vapor condenses on the discs, giving them a uniform coating about 100 nanometers thick.

The second method, called "sputtering," is also performed in a vacuum chamber

particles at this step as well. The acrylic layer is applied by a spin-coating machine and the entire disc is dried with ultraviolet light. After the covering dries, the label and disc information are silk-screened onto the surface.

Quality Control and Packaging

At this point the discs are essentially complete. They can be handled and carefully inspected. Part of the final inspection subjects each disc to a high-performance CD player called a Complete Disc Checker (CDC). This machine plays the entire CD at high speed, checking not only for sonic dropouts, but also for the operational digital codes, block data errors, warpage, and general problems with the tracks and pits themselves. Once a disc

and involves spraying the discs with a fine ion mist. An aluminum electrode is heated until it begins emitting electrically charged aluminum atoms which bond to the surface of the discs. In either method, the discs are evenly coated with a layer of reflective metal, usually aluminum, but occasionally silver or even gold.

This step of the manufacturing process yields the most defective discs since there is a high possibility of microscopic holes in the reflective surface. To catch such errors, a visual inspection and a series of automated tests are performed on every disc—all still within the confines of a clean room.

The final step is the sealing of the coated data surface with a layer of acrylic resin. Great care must be taken to prevent the sealing in of dust

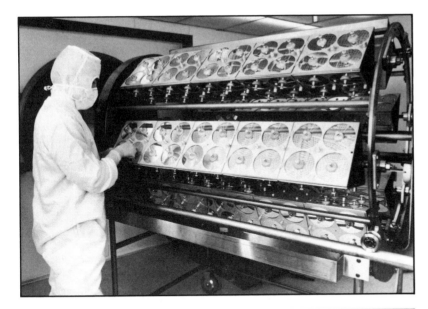

Vacuum deposition chamber. The discs shown here have just received the metallized reflective layer. Next, they receive a protective coating and printed label.

passes its quality control checks, it is packaged, boxed, and shipped off for distribution.

The rejection rate at CD plants can be very high, especially when the plant first begins operation. But as the personnel gain more experience and the manufacturing processes become refined, the rejection rate drops. Due to the rigorous testing of the disc, the defect rate of Compact Discs reaching the store is remarkably low, at least as compared to LPs and cassettes. In most cases, even discs which are returned prove to be playable, indicating random hardware problems rather than defective software.

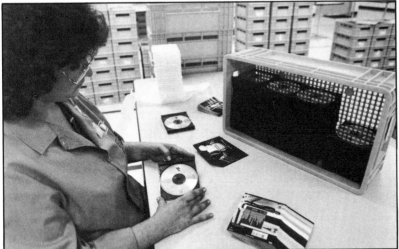

Final packaging of the discs.

VIDEODISC: THE CD'S OLDER COUSIN

The Compact Disc is not the first laser-read optical disc to reach the consumer market. That distinction belongs to the LaserVision videodisc, first introduced in the late 1970s. These 12-inch platters hold an hour of video (with sound track) on each side, making them suitable for distribution of movies. (They also come in an 8-inch variety, storing about 20 minutes of video per side.)

The LaserVision videodisc is sometimes confused with RCA's now defunct SelectaVision videodisc. SelectaVision was not an optical disc, but instead used a reading head that actually touched the

A LaserVision videodisc and player. The first optical-disc consumer product was the videodisc, which holds an hour of video per side.

groove of the disc, causing the disc to wear with successive playings.

In this respect, LaserVision videodiscs are like CDs: nothing touches the track of pits that hold the video information. But unlike CD's digital audio storage, the video signals encoded in the videodisc's pits are analog. For video, this turns out to be a more efficient way to store the signal. The videodisc spins at about three times the rate of a CD, and the resulting image is very high quality—better than normal VHS, Beta, or 8-mm videotape.

Unfortunately, video-tape, with its ability to record as well as play back, proved far more popular with consumers than the videodisc, which is a read-only medium. However, with the advent of CD, videodisc is making a comeback in several ways. First, the CD/LV combination players that can play both CDs and videodiscs have stimulated interest in both of these optical media. And second, videodiscs have recently gained the ability to store a digital audio soundtrack that is equivalent in quality to the CD.

This increased crossover between the technologies is now further enhanced by the introduction, in late 1987, of CD-Video (CD-V) format, a CD-sized disc that holds 20 minutes of CD digital audio and 5 minutes of analog video with a CD digital soundtrack. CD-V players will be able to play CD-V discs as well as regular CD-Audio discs. Some CD-V players will also accommodate the 8-inch and 12-inch videodiscs which have now been designated as CD-Video products. Manufacturers view the 5-inch CD-V as a convenient way to package the hits from a music album along with a single video clip for purchase by consumers.

CHAPTER 7

Music for the Compact Disc

The Compact Disc is a digital audio storage medium. But that does not necessarily mean that the source material stored there was originally recorded in digital form. In fact, the music on the majority of today's CDs was recorded on analog equipment and later transferred to the digital format. There are numerous outstanding CDs that originated in the analog domain.

However, the same sonic benefits of the CD digital storage medium—clean, clear sound—can be realized in the original studio recording environment by using digital equipment there. More and more studios are converting to digital as artists, produc-

ers, and engineers learn to get the most from this new medium.

DIGITAL RECORDING

As described in Chapter 2, digital audio involves the conversion of an analog sound waveform into digital data, which can then be stored on a Compact Disc. The actual conversion from analog to digital can occur at any of the three basic steps in the recording process: *recording*, *mixing*, or *mastering*.

The recording steps consist of capturing sounds on a recording medium such as

magnetic audio tape. This involves one of two basic recording approaches: 2-track or multitrack. (These are not sequential tracks as on a CD, but parallel tracks on audio recording tape.) Two-track recording—left channel and right channel for stereo—is well suited for live recording, when no further manipulation of the recorded instruments or voices will be required.

By comparison, multitrack recording may involve as many as 32 or 48 separate audio tracks. These tracks are synchronized so that the various musical elements of the recording—vocals, drums, instruments, etc.—can be isolated on separate tracks on

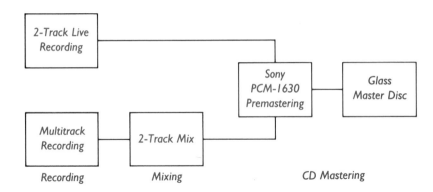

| 2-Track Live Recording | | Sony PCM-1630 Premastering | Glass Master Disc |
| Multitrack Recording | 2-Track Mix | | |

| Recording | Mixing | CD Mastering |

The three steps in the recording process. Most pop and rock music is recorded on multitrack machines and then mixed to 2-track. Many live classical performances are recorded directly on 2-track machines, bypassing the need for a mixing step. In either case, the final mastering step is the same.

the tape. In this way, tracks can be recorded independently at different times with attention to the unique audio characteristics of each element.

During the mixing process, these tracks are individually processed and carefully blended into a composite stereo image. This final mixed version of the multitrack recording is recorded, or *mixed down*, to a 2-track recording machine. (Since live, 2-track recordings are already in 2-track format, no mixing step is required.)

Multitrack and 2-track recording equipment is available in both analog and digital varieties, and the recording and mixing steps can be done in either analog or digital format. However, the mastering process for a CD is always digital. This step involves converting the audio from the 2-track mix or live recording to the exact digital format required for the CD.

Most experts and listeners agree that CDs usually benefit if all three processes take place in the digital domain. But a well-produced analog recording can often be turned into a quality CD. Likewise, an all-digital production will not make up for inferior ma-

terial, performance, or recording technique.

How can you tell just what the production steps have been on a CD? One way is to rely on the *SPARS code*. SPARS stands for the Society of Professional Audio Recording Studios, the group that originated the code. It is a three-letter code found on the cover of many CD packages, as well as on the label of the disc. The letters are either A or D and indicate which of the three steps—recording, mixing, and mastering—were analog and which were digital. (For CDs, the mastering step is always digital.) Relevant SPARS code combinations include:

AAD—Analog recording

and mixing; digital mastering. This typifies transfers from LPs where no extra digital processing occurred.

ADD—Analog recording; digital mixing and mastering. This type of disc is becoming more prevalent with the proliferation of affordable digital 2-track mixing equipment.

DDD—Digital all the way. This does not guarantee high-quality sound, but it greatly improves the chances.

DAD—Unusual combination of digital recording and analog mixing. If the producer went to the trouble and expense of recording digitally, it's unlikely that the mix would occur in analog.

Use of the SPARS system of coding is still being debated. Some critics charge that the code may mislead by providing too little information and overemphasizing the digital nature of any single step. For instance, no evaluation of the relative quality of the three steps is offered. Simply being digital doesn't guarantee optimum production. Badly produced digital processes have proven inferior to superbly produced analog processes in some instances.

Other critics maintain that the music itself should be the primary criterion in judging the quality of a disc. Many famous works by artists as diverse as Jascha Heifetz, Louis Armstrong, Elvis Presley, and the Beatles exist only on analog sources. Therefore, these products, even when successfully remastered to meet digital standards, still cannot carry a D in the first position of the SPARS code.

Consequently, not all labels use the code. Many simply report the information in plain language on the cover—for example, "analog recording / digital mix." In such cases, the manufacturer often doesn't bother to reiterate the digital nature of the mastering process. While details of the disc's production history may not tell the whole story, it is nonetheless advisable to refer to it when available.

The Benefits of Digital

It must first be said that not everyone agrees that digital recordings are better than analog ones. There are still critics, artists, and engineers alike who maintain that the digital mode is less "warm" than analog. They hear a certain harshness in the upper frequencies which they maintain is not present in well-made analog recordings. The very nature of digital recording could lend some credence to this claim. Chapter 2 described the sampling and quantization steps of the pulse code modulation process. It involves dividing a waveform into small, discrete segments that must be restored to their original smooth continuity by the output filtering of the CD player. Analog recording, on the other hand, emulates the continuous patterns of waveforms that some believe leads to a more natural-sounding result.

It must be pointed out, however, that this question encompasses broader issues as well. The relative skill of the recording engineers and the quality of their equipment play considerable roles in the final outcome of digital recordings. The CD has proven that it can offer a high degree of warmth and naturalness, as evidenced by the number of critics who are now openly enthusiastic about its benefits.

The overwhelming majority opinion remains that, in spite of minor tonal idiosyncrasies, the technological advantages of digital recording, mixing, and mastering far outweigh potential drawbacks. The primary benefit is the enhanced quality of the audio information due to the extremely precise representation of its detail.

Analog recording technique, for example, may require extensive adjustment of the frequency spectrum of a particular voice or instrument, a process called *equalization*. This compensates for uneven frequency response inherent in the analog medium. Further loss of quality arises from the continuous degradation of the audio information as the tape is passed across the recording and playback heads of the machine. Finally, analog suffers from the build-up of system-generated noise and tape hiss with each successive *generation*, or copy to another tape.

Digital audio, on the other hand, combines extremely low noise, an even frequency response, extended dynamic range, and absolutely no loss of quality in succeeding generations. When a digital recording is digitally copied, all the zeroes and ones are exactly reproduced. The copy is a precise replica of the original.

Since a number of generations are required in the process of transferring music from a master tape to the fi-

DIGITAL SYNTHESIZERS FOR CD MUSIC

Until the mid-1970s, computerized music synthesis was confined to well-funded research laboratories at Stanford, MIT, and other universities. Since then, digital synthesizers have proliferated at an amazing pace, from $50 keyboards in toy stores to $100,000 professional systems.

The Synclavier and the Fairlight CMI are two of the high-end digital synthesizers that can record, create, combine, and edit any number of sounds—either natural or synthesized. Both machines incorporate full-fledged computers that process sound stored in memory or on magnetic discs. ▶

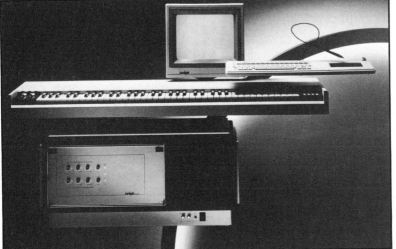

The Synclavier and the Fairlight CMI digital sampling synthesizers. Each machine offers extensive capabilities for digital recording, manipulation, and playback of any audio source.

Both of these keyboard-based digital-recording and -playback devices provide a powerful array of tools for the creation of electronic music. An artist like Laurie Anderson, for example, uses the Synclavier to sample (record) a sound, then analyze it, alter it, and play it back in its new form as part of a multi-track recording.

An excellent example is the rhythmic "shake, shake, shake-shake" modified vocal that begins "KoKoKu" on Anderson's *Mister Heartbreak* CD and continues throughout in the song's background. By "looping" this processed audio, the Synclavier creates a unique rhythm track that sounds like a blend of voice and sand blocks.

Not all sampled sounds need be vocal. Herbie Hancock used his two

Fairlight CMIs to produce many of the unusual sounds in his hit song "Rockit," from his *Future Shock* CD.

The source sound can be gathered in the field, recorded live onto disc, or taken directly from another digital source. Hancock used a Sony PCM-FI (a portable digital recorder) to gather the ethnic musical sounds and rhythms of Africa for his *Soundsystem* album. By processing the samples on the Fairlight and combining them with studio instruments, Hancock created an intriguing blend of acoustic and electronic tonalities.

nal disc—especially for multi-track efforts—this is a crucial issue. While analog copies lose quality at a fairly significant rate, it is theoretically possible to create an infinite number of successive genera-

tions of a digital recording with no perceptible loss of fidelity. No other medium offers the artist such consistently flawless reproduction of the original work.

The Digital Studio

One hundred years of analog recording techniques have established some deeply held attitudes about how a good recording is made. By 1980, state-of-the-art analog multitrack recording had become a thoroughly entrenched way of doing things in the music industry. The vast majority of the world's commercial music was, and continues to be, recorded in elaborately designed, independent studios which have invested heavily in analog multitrack equipment. The prospect, therefore, of redesigning and outfitting for digital multitrack capabilities initially met with some skepticism, if not outright resistance. Understandably so, since a 24-track digital re-

corder alone can cost well in excess of $100,000.

Yet, despite the inconvenience, expense, and risk involved in converting to digital, the trend has gathered momentum with surprising speed. In the beginning, digital recording was reserved primarily for classical-music projects. Since performance of classical repertoire can often be captured in simple right/left stereo format, it proved to be a natural ground for early experiments. Some of the earliest digital examples are 2-track live recordings of classical performances.

Another reason for this early symbiosis between classical and digital was the fact that many major classical record labels tended to do their own recording rather than contracting with independent studios. The larger classical labels could afford to experiment with digital techniques. The even frequency response and extended dynamic range, capable of capturing the pu-

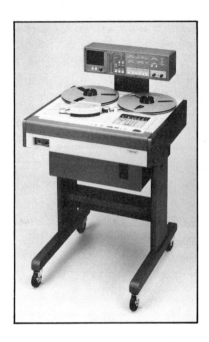

The Sony PCM-3402 2-track digital recorder. This type of unit is used both for live recording and for mixdown of multitrack recordings.

rity of the instrument tones and the ambience of the concert hall, were benefits clearly suited to classical projects. What's more, an enthusiastic support base of audiophile consumers already existed in the classical market.

Since standard analog recorders do not have sufficient bandwidth to accommodate the extended range of the digital audio signal plus the accompanying control data, a good deal of 2-track digital recording is done on ¾-inch video tape machines. These machines incorporate formats designed to handle the high frequencies involved in recording visual images. They easily encompass the bandwidth of digital signals and data streams. Digital encoding is typically done by means of a pulse code modulation (PCM) encoder which transforms the analog signal into digital data for storage on the video tape.

But 2-track recording will not suffice for most pop music. Such music tends to require the specialized techniques permitted by multitrack recording. The volume levels of the instruments require more isolation to prevent interference among their parts. Also, because of the complex acoustics of some electronic instruments, sepa-rate processing of individual parts is often required to achieve a blend of all the sounds represented on the recording.

To meet the specialized production needs of pop music, Sony and 3M were among the first to offer multitrack digital recorders. These 24- or 32-track machines were quite costly and suffered from early design problems. Later generations of machines saw significant improvements over earlier models and the entry of new contenders into the market, such as Mitsubishi of Japan. Today's digital recorders feature better synchronization circuitry and lower cost, thus bringing them more in line with current analog multitrack machines.

Most recording engineers agree that the trend toward more practical and less expensive digital multitrack recording is essential to its ultimate success as an industry standard. The last three years have seen an increase in the numbers of pop artists and

The Sony 3324 multitrack digital recorder. This unit records up to 24 parallel audio tracks on magnetic tape.

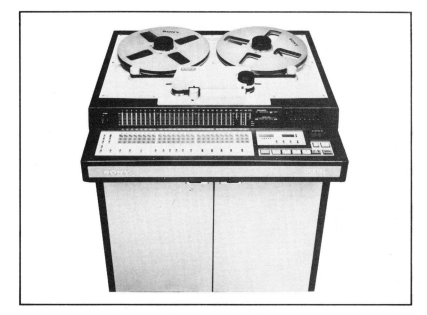

producers choosing to record digitally. As CD sales continue to surge, artists and labels interested in producing digital recordings will certainly continue to grow. As a result, the cost to an independent multitrack studio of "going digital" will become more justifiable.

Regardless of whether the recording and mixing are done in analog or digital, the third and final step of the process of getting sound on a CD—mastering—must be done in the digital domain. CD mastering involves two steps. The first one is *premastering*, in which the 2-track live recording or mixdown is digitized with a

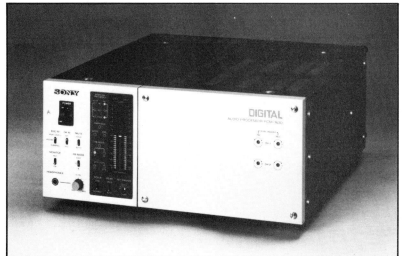

The Sony PCM-1630 digital audio processor. The 1630, and its predecessor, the Sony PCM-1610, are the industry-standard professional units for converting audio into the CD digital format during premastering.

PCM encoder to the Compact Disc audio standard.

This encoder converts the audio to the 16-bit, 44.1-kHz sampling format required for storage on Compact Disc. The standard medium for premastering is, once again, the ¾-inch video tape. During encoding, the tape is also annotated with the time codes that mark the beginning and ending of each track on the CD. The tape is then sent to the CD pressing plant for the second mastering step: the making of the glass master disc, as described in Chapter 6.

DO-IT-YOURSELF DIGITAL RECORDING

Digital Audio appeared in the home entertainment market as early as 1977 when Sony introduced the PCM-1—the world's first digital audio processor. The device made it possible to transform regular analog audio signals into digitally encoded audio information, store it on standard video cassettes using a standard video cassette recorder (VCR), and play it back through any stereo system.

Shortly thereafter, the Electronic Industries Association of Japan (EIAJ) issued a set of standards for devices using digital audio recording and playback. The move opened the door for the creation of the audio Compact Disc and firmly entrenched digital audio processors as essential tools in the digital recording industry.

PCM units are now quite common and affordable (under $1000), and are sold by a number of manufacturers. PCM stands for *pulse code modulation*, the technique discussed in Chapter 2 by which binary pulses are recorded on tape to create digital codes used to store audio digitally.

Video tape was chosen as the medium because its wide video-signal bandwidth was ideal for the requirements of digital audio. The entire width of the tape is used to record the audio signals.

Since all magnetic tapes suffer from dropouts—glitches in the oxide coating which prevent accurate recording in spots—PCM units utilize standard error-correction techniques. PCM recordings are high-quality digital recordings that offer the same full range of sonic quality you get with a Compact Disc.

Some PCM units, such as the Sony PCM-F1, are sold with an optional companion VCR—in the case of the PCM-F1, it is the Sony SL-2000. But any VCR may be used with any PCM processor, including either Beta or VHS. The combined Sony units weigh less than 18 pounds and in addition to standard AC operation can be powered with battery packs or a car/boat battery adapter. This makes the PCM an ideal unit for field and location recording, as well as home taping.

The selectable speeds found on most VCR decks can be used to obtain from two to six hours of recording time. The sampling rate of 44.1 kHz remains the same regardless of the speed chosen, but the increased density of data on the tape with the longer playing times can lead to more errors in the data.

Any audio signal may be fed into the PCM processor through either a microphone with a ¼-inch

phone plug or standard RCA stereo connectors. While PCM processors are routinely used in professional applications, they are equally practical and popular as home units. For instance, LP collections can be digitally archived on video tape using a PCM processor.

Home recordists can also use the PCM unit as a digital mixing deck in combination with home multitrack recording systems such as those from Tascam and Fostex. The

The Sony PCM-601ESD, a consumer digital audio processor. Used in conjunction with a home video cassette recorder, this type of unit can store and play back sound in digital format.

PCM gives musicians the capability to do professional-quality digital mixing at home for a fraction of the price most studios charge. And, since no quality loss takes place when digital copies are made (unlike analog copying), you can join two machines together to make virtually unlimited high-quality copies.

Digital technology has resulted in the potential for vast improvements in the sound quality of consumer recordings. The CD you listen to at home can deliver a level of audio quality usually found only on the master recordings made in the sound studio.

In the final analysis, it is the record companies which bear the responsibility for the quality of the product they issue on CD. Since the standards and criteria may vary from label to label, it is perhaps worth considering the roles the labels play in deciding what you get on disc and just how reliable it may be.

RECORD LABELS

The earliest labels to become involved with Compact Disc technology were those which had the greatest interest in its success. PolyGram, a subsidiary of Philips, produced many of the first commercially available CDs. CBS Records, which at that time had a working relationship with Sony, also produced some of the early CDs.

The way had been paved by a growing number of consumers interested in higher-quality sound. These so-called audiophiles were investing in the best and latest equipment, and they wanted recordings that would show off the capabilities of their new systems. By the late 1970s, many audiophile labels, catering to the high-end audio market, were already experimenting with improved LP techniques. A process called *direct-to-disk* recording had already yielded significantly better phonograph discs. This approach bypassed the tape medium altogether using direct signals from the microphones to cut tracks in the master disc. This master was used to press the LPs which therefore reflected only one generation of copying.

Their production, however, imposed severe limits on the flexibility of the recording session. Each side of the master disc had to be recorded from beginning to end as a live performance, with no editing possible. Given the industry's reliance on multitrack recording, the direct-to-disk method had limited appeal to many musicians and engineers.

A more significant development perhaps was the appearance of LP versions of digital recordings. Although still prone to the problems inherent to the LP—primarily noise and wear—these discs clearly advanced awareness of the advantages of digital technology. In a sense, they helped provide a bridge for consumers to the forthcoming optical disc.

When Compact Discs first appeared, the audiophile labels—most of which were classically oriented—were among the first to make them available. In fact, many of the earliest CDs to appear on the market were reissues of those very same live classical performances that had been recorded digitally in the late 1970s. Classical-music fans appreciated the vastly improved sonic performance. Digitally recorded CDs were capable of capturing not only the intimate details of the performance—a finger squeaking on a violin string, the expressive breathing of a concert pianist—but also the subtle feeling of being in the concert hall. All this, combined with the CD's unprecedented durability, created an eager demand for the new discs and players.

With the exception of Poly-Gram and CBS, however, many of the larger record labels were still less than enthusiastic about a new music format—especially considering the heavy investment required for manufacturing facilities. Moreover, in 1984 and 1985, it seemed uncertain to many of these companies whether CD would really catch on as a mainstream consumer medium.

The turning point came in the 1985 Christmas season, when enough popular CDs had reached the market to cause player sales to sky-rocket. Many hi-fi stores sold completely out of CD players. This buying frenzy convinced the major labels to make a full commitment to the Compact Disc. The number of titles available has risen from fewer than two thousand in early 1984 to as many as 15,000 by the end of 1987.

Music For Everyone

All along, records have only been as popular as the artists represented on the medium. The early Edison machines and discs remained toys for the wealthy until two things happened: first, they became mass produced and affordable; and second, artists such as Enrico Caruso and W.C. Handy began appearing on phonograph. For many music lovers, this was the first opportunity to hear artists previously heard only in concert halls and vaude-

ville houses.

The same has been true of the CD. Every month since the advent of the CD, the music press has been filled with news of more and more artists—both contemporary and historic—available on disc. A survey of categories and discs on the market currently reveals a surprising array of choices for a medium only five years old.

The initial hesitancy on the part of major labels gave way by the beginning of 1985. Although classical discs were responsible for the bulk of the catalog for the first few years, by mid-1987 pop selections were accounting for the majority of CD sales. As production at disc-manufacturing plants increased, a flurry of new CD releases has hit the pop and rock market.

Still, even the more aggressive attitudes have proven insufficient to meet demand in some cases. The landmark CD release in 1985 of Dire Straits' *Brothers in Arms* was one of Warner

A FULL CD'S WORTH OF MUSIC

74 minutes and 33 seconds —that's the practical limit on the amount of stereo audio that a CD can hold. The story goes that when Philips was considering the size of the Compact Disc, conductor Herbert von Karajan was asked how much music one of these new discs should hold. His reputed reply was that it should be long enough to accommodate his recording of Beethoven's Fifth Symphony, which plays for about 72 minutes. Thus the CD's size was set.

Most LPs hold no more than 45 minutes of music, and many have little more than a half hour on them. Since most of the programming for Compact Discs is taken directly from material that is also released in LP and cassette versions, it's the rare CD that approaches the upper limit of its storage capacity.

However, several encouraging trends for getting the maximum music on a disc are becoming evident. First is the appearance of more and more classical discs with increased playing time. Coming close to the edge is the Denon release of Bruckner's Eighth Symphony conducted by Lovro von Matičič, which plays for 74 minutes and 13 seconds. One reason for the particular interest classical labels have shown in increased playing time is that there are no royalties paid to composers now long deceased.

The same is not true for the songwriters of recent popular music. The more songs on a disc, the more the record label must pay in music-publishing royalties. Motown Records has issued a number of "two-fer" CDs, with the music from two original LP albums on a single disc. The label was able to do this economically because it also owns the publishing rights to most of the music released on those CDs.

As more material is developed exclusively for the Compact Disc format, you're likely to see many of those titles exceed the 60-minute barrier.

Bros. Records' first major international CD marketing efforts. An initial 200,000 discs were distributed to outlets, all of which sold out in short order. Industry analysts speculated that twice as many could have been sold.

In addition to current best-seller releases, a host of older albums with proven track

records were rushed to the market as well. Pink Floyd's *Dark Side of the Moon*, on *Billboard* magazine's Top-200 list for 13 years, was one of the earliest releases of an established album on CD. Currently, most new major LP releases are distributed simultaneously on cassette and CD. As player sales increase, older vintage recordings, as well, are appearing with the same regularity.

The classical market continues to be a dependable source for CD sales, even spurring interest among new and younger buyers. Since the classical market had a head start in digital recording, classical CDs have helped set the standards for quality and excellence. Labels such as Telarc, Denon, and Delos have successfully concentrated on producing classical discs. And established classical labels such as CBS's Masterworks and RCA's Red Seal have begun issuing impressive CD collections as well.

Jazz is the third largest CD group. Like classical, many jazz projects had been digitally recorded in recent years. Since jazz fans have also traditionally paid the price for audiophile recordings, the labels tried early test runs of jazz CDs. The jazz market has been the center of considerable interest in vintage remastering, as well, and selections now range from historic blues and jazz to the latest works of artists such as Wynton Marsalis and Flim and the BBs.

A number of other category bins are now appearing in CD stores. In fact, almost every major music style is respectably represented on CD. Neglected in early CD releases, country music is catching up with the rest of the pack, mostly represented by the more popular artists. The Easy Listening section goes from early Sinatra, to Lawrence Welk, to the Mys-

Classical CD hits. Classical music led the way for consumer acceptance of the Compact Disc.

Jazz CD hits. Jazz music has found wide acceptance among CD owners conscious of high quality.

tic Moods Orchestra, and incorporates recordings by newer artists, such as Michael Rogers' *Digital Steel* on steel drums. Many movie soundtracks and original cast performances are now available on Compact Disc as well.

A growing International Section includes traditional music from folk ensembles and performers from many countries, often on small folk labels from within the countries. Especially interesting is the release of a series of Compact Discs on the Mobile Fidelity label of selected material from Melodiya, the official record label of the Soviet Union.

Some of the most impressive and accessible world music, however, is found in the bins labeled New Age. This category has appeared only in this decade, pioneered by labels such as Windham Hill which has a dedication to intelligent, non-intrusive music. Although labeled by some critics as

"Nutrasweet Muzak," it nevertheless has continued to gather a strong, supportive following. New Age appeals to a broad spectrum of buyers, many of whom have tired of high-energy rock and roll. Typical discs might include anything from an album of George Winston piano solos, to Paul Winter's live, on-location ode to life in the Grand Canyon, entitled *Canyon*, to New Age musicians from around the world, such as the Swiss harpist Andreas Vollenweider.

The Old and The New

Recently, one of the most exciting and long-awaited developments on the CD market has been the reappearance of vintage recordings on CD. These discs are often the result of a number of advances in the digital *remastering* process.

Older analog master tapes have recently been determined to have a shelf life of about twenty-five years. After that time, the tape's oxide coating may begin to deteriorate, resulting in blistered, cracked, and peeling sections. Some of the most prized recording sessions of the last 50 years have become unusable for all practical purposes. This has made the technique of digital remastering of great interest to the record labels.

Such restructuring techniques tend to require slow, painstaking effort. The remastering process begins with the transfer of the analog tapes to digital format. A digital PCM copy is carefully made from the original recording and renovated to its fullest extent using standard digital processing techniques. The mastering process is then carried out using the new digital master.

If the original analog master tape is seriously flawed, missing or damaged portions can be reconstructed using other sections of the same recording. Since digital audio can be manipulated as numerical data, editing and data manipulation can be extremely precise. Tiny fragments of sound from other locations on the tape can be sampled, digitally altered to approximate the sound of missing sections, and used to bridge the gaps in the deteriorated recording.

First, single sound units, such as individual syllables or single instrument tones, are isolated. They are then electronically altered in pitch, tempo, and coloration to match the material they are replacing. By averaging the numerical values of the sound before and after the missing section, a tonal bridge can be created which closely resembles the data that were originally there.

Specialty Discs

Some of the earliest types of CDs released were *samplers*, collections of music by various artists, usually from one label. Popular samplers from Denon, Telarc, Arista, Motown, GRP, and Windham Hill helped introduce many new listeners to the Compact Disc. Originally intended as enticements for new CD buyers, CD samplers continue to sell well. Another popular way to get music from various artists is to buy movie soundtrack music on CD. Several hundred have been released.

Other specialized categories of audio are becoming available on CD as well. This includes spoken-word discs such as plays, vintage radio collections, and writers reading their own works. You'll even find a Vatican release on the Deutsche Grammophon label with Pope John Paul II celebrating a Solemn High Mass at St. Peter's.

Some of the first educational CDs—foreign language discs in Spanish and French from Conversa-phone—appeared in 1987. Each 2-disc set includes a complete instruction booklet. The company advertises the fact that you can repeat selected segments *ad infinitum*, thanks to the CD format.

THE BEATLES ON COMPACT DISC

Ever since the CD first appeared, fans have wondered when the Beatles' music would come packaged in a jewel box. In 1985, a CD version of *Abbey Road* was released for distribution in Japan only. But copies found their way into this country and began to stimulate demand for the "Fab Four" on CD. The record company promptly discontinued the disc, citing disputes over royalties to be paid for the new format. The *Abbey Road* CD became a collector's item, seen advertised for as much as $100 in audio magazine classified ads.

The suspense finally ended on February 26, 1987, when the first four Beatles albums hit store shelves across America. These included *Please, Please Me*, *With The Beatles*, *A Hard Day's Night*, and *Beatles For Sale*, all issued in the original configurations as released in Great Britain on the Parlophone label. And all in *monophonic* sound, as originally recorded.

It turns out that the record label—EMI—delayed the CD versions primarily because they wanted to guarantee adequate supply for the expected intense demand for these discs. The demographic profile of a majority of CD owners matches that of people who grew up listening to Beatles music.

George Martin, producer of all the Beatles' records, was involved in supervising and approving the transfer to CD not only of the first four albums but also the eight subsequent ones that made their appearance—in stereo—during the months that followed. Perhaps the most eagerly awaited Beatles album, *Sgt. Pepper's Lonely Hearts Club Band*, appeared on June 1, 1987—the twentieth anniversary of its original appearance in 1967. "It was twenty years ago today, Sgt. Pepper taught the band to play. . . ."

The first four Beatles albums on Compact Disc. The remainder of the long-awaited CD versions of the Beatles' music appeared throughout 1987.

The repeat feature may also be used in conjunction with environmental and sound effects discs to create ambient sound backgrounds. A digital recording of bird calls in an early morning meadow, for instance, can be repeated softly in a room to provide a realistic feeling of outdoors.

Specialty discs also include children's discs, ranging from *Le Petit Prince* to George Winston and Meryl Streep's version of *The Velveteen Rabbit*. Also appearing are comedy discs with a number of major comedians such as Bill Cosby, George Carlin, and

Spoken-word CDs. A variety of audio material is now appearing on CD, including foreign-language training, interactive mysteries, fitness workouts, narrated stories, and religious services.

Richard Pryor. And, of course, you can get Jane Fonda's aerobic workout on CD.

And at least two *new* categories have been spawned by the CD. The first is *test discs*, which may include sound effects, music, and test tones to help you put your player through its paces. The second category, truly in its infancy, is the *interactive audio disc.* The broadway soundtrack to *The Mystery of Edwin Drood* features a multiple-ending scenario that offers the listener a hand in the proceedings. You can choose which of the characters you believe to be guilty of the central crime by programming your player to play specific ending tracks. In other words, you take a hand in devising the ending to the mystery.

CD-ONLY "RECORD" LABELS

In the last few years, some of the most remarkable support for the CD format has come not from the major labels, but from a number of small independent start-ups which are interested in producing only CDs. Unencumbered by the massive organizational weight of the larger companies, and free from the expense of producing multiple formats, the CD-only labels have been held back only by the shortage of disc pressing capacity. Since many of the larger labels own or wield powerful influence with the plants, the smaller companies have been forced to wait in line. Despite the production shortage, companies such as Delos and Rykodisc have won the respect and support of CD buyers because of their unique offerings and their stringent commitment to the quality of the medium.

Delos is primarily a classical record label, in business since the mid-1970s. Guided by the sure management hand of Amelia Haygood, Delos has produced dozens of quality classical recordings in tape, LP, and CD. But as the CD surge began to overpower the analog formats for classical music, Delos recognized the beginning of the end for nondigital music. In 1986, the label ceased production of tapes and LPs and now issues CDs only.

A new company called Rykodisc bills itself as "the record company that doesn't make records." All of its over 35 releases since 1984 have been on Compact Disc only, with many containing over 60 minutes of sound. The Rykodisc catalog is an eclectic collection of pop, jazz, folk, reggae, environmental sounds, and rock, including 10 discs by Frank Zappa.

CHAPTER 8

CD Software Buyer's Guide

With your CD player at home and installed, you are ready for what may be the best part of converting to digital audio: beginning your CD collection. Sounds easy you say? It is, but thinking the process through, step by step, will help guarantee satisfaction with your investment and ensure your continued enjoyment. After all, the higher prices of Compact Discs demand a thoughtful approach to selecting your purchases.

With over ten thousand titles now available and the range of American and international labels rapidly expanding, it is a safe bet that you will never lack for interesting and innovative CDs. Just as the LP has become a presence in homes around the world, the CD will likely follow suit. And as prices drop and CD-carrying outlets proliferate, finding the discs you want—and staying within your budget—will become as easy as buying LPs.

Shopping for CDs can be great fun, especially if you feel secure about choosing the right discs. You should end a CD shopping spree feeling that you bought quality discs for a reasonable price. The added factors involved in evaluating CDs—relative sound quality, amount of material on the disc, and its production history—provide guidelines you may never have used when buying LPs.

Most people become interested in buying a recording through recommendations of friends, by hearing it on radio or TV or reading a review, or by seeing it on display in the store. When you find a disc that interests you, ask yourself these three simple questions:

1. Is it a quality disc?
2. Is the price fair?

3. Where is the best place to buy it?

Of course, the material on the disc, the recording artist, and the quality of the performance are considerations which may justify purchase at any price. But even then you may find that intelligent shopping will result in better value. For instance, if you are interested in a recording of Vivaldi's "Four Seasons," you can find more than thirty CD versions of it on various labels and by various ensembles. A bit of comparative research could mean the difference between buying a "ho-hum" gatherer of shelf dust and an exciting disc which becomes an important part of your collection.

EVALUATING DISCS

There are many ways you can evaluate a disc before purchasing it. As always, your best guide is your own ear. If possible, listen to the disc in person before buying it. If you know someone who owns the disc, it should be relatively easy to hear it or at least get a personal opinion. If that is not possible, try to hear the disc at a retail outlet.

This may not be as difficult as it sounds. The CD's durability makes active previewing a more reasonable possibility than with the LP. With each subsequent play of an LP, a bit of the quality is lost. Consequently, retail outlets have rarely allowed customers to preview LPs on an individual basis. This is proving not to be the case with the CD. In fact, some CD-only stores now offer a special previewing area, outfitted with players and headphones, where you can listen to many of the CDs they offer.

Other retail outlets may play the disc for you by request over the house system, or provide alternative facilities for individual listening.

Some Chicago-area stores, for instance, have incorporated the Seeburg Corporation's new CD Jukeboxes (see Chapter 9) in an innovative approach to the problem. Customers can preview up to 60 different discs per jukebox, using eight pairs of attached headphones, without ever having to touch the discs.

If you can't manage to hear the CD in person, you may find that the radio is a helpful ally. Most stations actively support CD awareness by pointing out when a Compact Disc is being played. Admittedly, this option has its limitations. For one, the frequency range of most FM broadcasting stations under the best conditions extends only to about 15 kHz. This means that radio cannot accurately represent the upper quarter of the CD's frequency response capabilities. Nonetheless, it can give you a very good idea of the content and quality of performance on the disc.

Guidelines for Listening

Regardless of how or when you finally hear the CD, there are standard criteria to use in evaluating a disc's sonic quality. As you have read in previous chapters, most CD players vary little in sound quality—most reproduce equally well the discs played on them. The CDs themselves, however, vary widely, reflecting the disparities in quality of the original source material.

The objective of all recording is to capture and reproduce as accurately as possible the original sounds in the true spirit of the performance. The success of the recording depends on the quality of the audio equipment as well as on the skill and experience of the engineers and technicians. A CD of a poorly made analog recording will never exhibit the sonics found on a well-made, all-digital recording.

While the subtleties of

Listening area in a CD store. Listening before buying is now practical with the Compact Disc, since the discs don't wear out with repeated playings. A good CD store should offer you this option.

sound quality may be difficult to evaluate on first try, with a little practice in critical listening you should be able to distinguish a good recording from a poor one. Various aspects of "good sound" have already been dealt with in this book; the same principles involved in evaluating the sound of a CD player apply here as well. Distortion, background hiss, hum, and other extraneous noise are usually indications of a less-than-perfect master recording. Such sonic prob-

lems can be quite irritating if significantly present. While they may not automatically qualify a CD as undesirable (the content of the disc, after all, may be more important than the sound quality), you will feel better if you know what to listen for.

First of all, you should be able to hear a well-balanced

representation of the frequency spectrum, from the lowest to the highest audible tones. The high end (5–20 kHz) should be crisp and clear. This portion of the frequency spectrum puts the *sizzle* in the sound. In pop recordings, this range is usually most evident in such instruments as the upper percussion (e.g., high-hat cymbals, tambourines) and synthesizers. In classical recordings, it is most noticeable in the strings and woodwinds. Distortion in the high end tends to be harsh and abrasive. An abundance of high-end distortion can seriously detract from the listening experience and contribute to *listener fatigue*.

The mid-range (100 Hz–5 kHz) represents the broad spectrum of textures and colors found in various musical timbres—the personalities of the instruments and the vocals reside here. The characteristics of the mid-range can be expressed in various ways. As a rule, it is com-

monly said that a well-balanced mid-range accounts for the naturalness of sound in a recording. Listen for realistic sounding voices and instruments. Ask yourself, "Does this sound live or canned?" When the mid-range is well represented, it lends a feeling of live warmth and intimacy to the recording.

The low end (below 100 Hz), in particular, sets the CD's capabilities apart from its analog predecessors. The low end on a good CD will be round and powerful. The bass guitar, the string basses, the low percussion (e.g., kick drum, tom-toms), and low organ tones on a good CD are felt as much as heard, gently but quite literally vibrating your chest and torso. It should be neither distorted nor muddy and formless; rather, lively, punchy, and clearly discernible.

Equally important to the effect of a quality recording is the feeling of spatial relationship within the sound. The

imaging, or distribution, of the sound in the listening space should contribute to a feeling of a live performance. On any good state-of-the-art recording, the imaginary performance stage between your speakers should have a sense of depth, with the space between the instruments clearly implied. The instruments should not sound crowded together in a blurred region somewhere in the center.

Finally, in the softest passages, there should be a minimum of extraneous sound. Hiss, rumble, or noise during the periods of silence is either left over from bad master tapes or reflects poor mastering. In any case, such distractions become more annoying with repeated listening—and as your familiarity with well-produced digital audio grows.

Information contained in the SPARS code can help you better interpret exactly what you're hearing. For instance, if you know that the original recording or mixing took place on analog equipment, you will have some clue as to the level of quality that can reasonably be expected. You would not be surprised, for instance, to notice some tape hiss or background noise during the quieter passages. Although the use of analog techniques certainly does not disqualify a CD as a good buy, it does indicate that it is more prone to sonic problems than if digital techniques had been used.

It is important to note that the recentness of the production is a crucial factor as well. If you are considering buying a remastering of a vintage Presley album, you can expect a certain amount of residual analog problems to be present—though they may be acceptable because of the historic nature of the content. On the other hand, if you play a CD of a recent, well-produced analog recording, you might have to listen very carefully to distinguish it from a digital recording.

As a rule, an all-digital (DDD) Compact Disc can be counted on to be quite satisfactory. Here, some knowledge of the label's reputation may be useful. Many labels devoted exclusively to digital recording—Telarc, dmp, and Denon, for instance—have a tradition of audiophile excellence. In addition, if you are familiar with the work of the producers or engineers credited on the cover, this may provide you with dependable clues as to what to expect.

Expert Opinions

If all attempts to hear the disc prove futile, there are other very useful alternatives. Promotional material and advertisements by the label— both in the store and in music periodicals like *Rolling Stone*—can be useful indicators of a disc's worth. In addition to giving you information about the disc's contents, such sources usually incorporate graphics and artwork

from the cover. If you haven't seen a copy of the disc, this may provide you with a sense of its mood and tone.

More thorough sources, however, are disc reviews appearing regularly in record and CD magazines. Reviews can be useful even if you have heard the disc yourself. The opinion of a critical listener can confirm your own reactions or uncover points you may have missed.

Reviews are also valuable because they let you quickly scan a large selection of discs. Monthly periodicals provide information on the very latest releases, while compilations and quarterly or yearly guides typically offer short capsule reviews of many previous releases. Different magazines cater to different tastes. Some are devoted exclusively to classical or jazz recordings, while others offer listings for all categories. Make sure you find those that match your particular interests.

Of course, variables such

as the reviewer's personal tastes and the audio equipment used by the reviewer should be taken into consideration. If the reviewer listens to discs on a top-quality stereo system, he or she may hear details that might be missed on more modest equipment.

Price of the Disc

A very practical factor in evaluating a disc is the cost. With most CDs costing between $10 and $15, you can spend over a hundred dollars for only ten discs. For shoppers accustomed to bringing home 10 LPs for perhaps one-third of that amount, the first trip to the CD store can be a bit dismaying.

While some single discs may appear for less than $10, many multidisc packages cost upwards of $50. Bargain-conscious buyers may be misled by such prices. Does a low price tag automatically signal good value? Are exor-

DISC REVIEW SOURCES

With the price of most Compact Discs running between $10 and $15, you want to have as much information as possible about a potential addition to your collection before purchasing it. If you can't preview the disc in the store or listen to a friend's copy, the best alternative is to turn to published reviews. In fact, even if you have heard the disc already, it is often helpful to see what insights reviewers can offer that you may have missed.

In most retail listening situations, you may not be able to hear the entire disc. The review can supplement what your ears tell you with useful information about the production, contents, and musicianship found on the disc.

Ideally, a review is the result of more than one careful listening session on the part of an experienced ear. A considered evaluation may save you dollars misspent on a disappointing product.

The following is a list of some recognized and dependable review sources. The majority of these can be found on newsstands or at most larger record stores.

Audio—Monthly magazine for audio enthusiasts. Features consumer-oriented reviews of equipment and recordings.

Digital Audio and Compact Disc Review—The first U.S. publication devoted entirely to Compact Disc and related equipment and issues. Features extensive reviews of the latest releases in all categories. Appears monthly.

Gramophone—Britain's ▶

most popular and thorough monthly review magazine. Specializes in classical but also includes some other styles. Very useful source of information about European imports which may be less well known in the U.S.

Green CD Catalog—The bimonthly listing of all available CD releases. Published by *Digital Audio and Compact Disc Review* and includes capsule reviews from past issues of that magazine.

High Fidelity—A monthly magazine specializing in audio equipment. Technical articles and reviews of both hardware and software are regularly featured.

Opus—A bimonthly listing of classical titles.

Ovation—A monthly listing of classical titles.

Rolling Stone—The leading music and pop-culture magazine in the U.S. Features articles on rock musicians and news of their recent projects. Includes reviews of many current pop and rock releases.

Schwann CD Catalog—The complete *Schwann Catalog* has long been one of the most thorough listings of phonograph recordings in the world. The first issue of their new Compact Disc supplement appeared in the fall of 1985. It is issued quarterly.

Stereo Review—A monthly magazine devoted to articles and reviews concerning audio equipment. Includes reviews of current releases of recordings in all styles.

Stevenson Compact Disc Review Guide—A quarterly review of approximately 160 pages that compiles ratings and reviews from many of the above sources.

bitantly priced packages worth the investment?

Once again, there are no easy answers. Your best approach is to use the criteria outlined earlier to make your first evaluation. Bargain-rate discs sometimes feature little-known performers or ensembles. On the other hand, they may simply be saving costs by using less elaborate packaging. Expensive multi disc collections may offer large symphonic works, such as Benjamin Britten's *War Requiem*, or complete performances of operas and musicals. If such works represent unusually superb performances or outstanding recording quality, they may be well worth the $60 to $70 price tag.

The higher cost of CDs is an issue that invariably arises in deciding whether to convert to digital audio. Music consumers who are still unfamiliar with the benefits of CD and CD players often cannot justify the move away from LPs for purely economical reasons. Even enthusiastic CD fans wonder why the large price differentials are necessary.

Actually, the additional cost is not unreasonable when you consider the investment required to create this new medium. First came the expense of funding the immense research and development effort Compact Disc technology required. Next followed the costs of designing and building—from scratch—enough high-tech manufacturing plants to handle the overnight increase in customer demand. Finally, consider the costs of converting older analog material to CD, implementing new forms of packaging, and creating marketing and advertising campaigns to educate the public about the new medium, and you might be forced to agree with industry representatives that the price of a CD is really quite a good deal.

Still, in the long run, less expensive discs invariably mean higher sales and more

thorough saturation of the market—all in the best interests of those who set the prices. In March 1987, one of the largest American CD plants cut prices more than 20 percent for its regular customers. And budget-priced lines are already routinely offered by major labels such as PolyGram, CBS, RCA, and MCA Classics.

As production and manufacturing techniques are perfected and more capacity becomes available, price cuts will become feasible, and much of those savings will be passed along to consumers. The CD industry expects that once the $10 average list price barrier is firmly broken, the CD will spread to all segments of music consumers.

For now you must simply be consoled by the fact that your additional dollars continue to underwrite development costs while buying you the best of one hundred years' worth of recording technology.

WHERE TO BUY THEM

It seems that just a few years ago you couldn't even find CDs at some major record shops. Now even your local grocery store may carry them. The number of sources for purchasing CDs and the accessories that go with them seems to grow daily.

Unlike questions involved in buying the players, disc purchases are fairly straightforward. The pros and cons of buying through chain outlets, independent stores, CD-only shops, mail-order companies, used-CD outlets, or CD-of-the-Month clubs have mostly to do with price, selection, and convenience. While large chain outlets may offer dependable supplies of the most popular CDs—as well as discount prices—they often provide less helpful services than more specialized stores.

CD-only stores, for instance, typically go to greater lengths to cater to you as an important new type of music buyer. They tend to promote CD shopping as a unique and fun experience. If you find one that provides individual listening areas and libraries of previewable discs, you can browse at your leisure, taking time to find discs with which you are likely to be happy.

CD-only outlets, by concentrating on CD products, typically provide a more eclectic variety of unusual and surprising discs than larger full-service record stores. A wide selection does not always equate with adequate stock, however. You may find that less common discs, generally unavailable at larger stores, will disappear quickly from the shelves of the specialized store. An interesting disc you discover at a CD-only shop might be out-of-stock there only a few days later. Less deviation from suggested list price can also be expected at CD-only outlets.

Customer support, essential when purchasing a CD player, can still be important when choosing a retailer from which to buy your discs. The chances are slim that you will ever need to return a defective disc, but it can happen. Due to differences in internal circuitry between players, for instance, minor disc flaws have been known to disrupt play on some machines but not others. Thus, you might conceivably find a disc which mistracks on your player at home, but performs perfectly on a test player at the store. In most cases, another copy of the same CD will function just fine on your player.

Should such a situation arise, you will want prompt and courteous treatment from the place you bought the disc. Any reputable dealer should recognize the problem immediately and replace it without hesitation. Stores that have less experience with CDs, however, might not fully understand such specialized problems and refuse to exchange the disc.

Compact Disc mail-order houses, which advertise regularly in audio magazines and buyer's guides, may vary widely in the degree of customer support they offer. As always, when you shop by mail you take certain chances in return for the convenience involved. While savings on software may not be impressive by mail (unless you order large quantities), such outlets offer extensive selection as well as a handy source for consumers who live in small towns and rural areas.

CD-of-the-Month clubs are also beginning to appear, offering the same benefit for buyers in outlying areas. They usually offer attractive savings as part of introductory offers, followed with consistent, up-to-date selections of the latest releases.

Until recently, imported CDs were a popular source

of works unavailable through American labels. Releases from Japan and Europe, especially, reflected the head start their recording industries had on the American market. Until 1985, almost all CDs were produced in either Japan or West Germany. Recent advances in manufacturing and production inside the U.S., however, are making it less necessary to turn to imports for adequate supplies of discs. Imported CDs are of interest now primarily for the rich array of material found outside this country. Foreign labels often take a more daring approach than labels here, resulting in innovative and very-high-quality releases. For this reason alone, a browse through the import bins in larger stores or in mail-order listings can be well worth your while.

Interestingly enough, the outlets that may profit most from the CD are the second-hand record stores. While these establishments have ex-

isted for a number of years selling used LPs and tapes, they have suddenly gained a new popularity with the advent of the durable CD. Since LPs and tapes have a much shorter lifespan, buyers at such shops necessarily sacrificed quality for cheap prices and unusual titles. With the CD, however, most used discs in good condition sound just as good as new ones.

Although used CDs don't sell as cheaply as used LPs, the benefits are strikingly obvious. If you tire of your old, less-favored CDs, simply take them in and trade them for ones you like better. You might receive as much as a third of the retail price of your old discs, depending on their marketability. This can be taken in credit toward other discs, new or used, which can be found in the same store. Average prices of used discs run between $8 and $12.

Incidentally, second-hand outlets can possibly provide a

is what makes a store like this so attractive to the avid buyer. You can spend hours scouring the CD bins before you exhaust all the possibilities.

Silver Platters also lets you "test-listen" any of over five hundred discs available for this purpose. A number of top-of-the-line CD players are available with high-quality headphones, so you can judge a disc by its sound.

In addition to the wide selection of discs, Silver Platters offers many types of CD accessories, including storage containers, carrying cases, and disc-cleaning kits. And Baker is not content to stop at the audio version of the Compact Disc. He promises to keep his customers on the CD leading edge by offering titles in CD-Video and CD-Interactive (discussed in Chapter 10) when they become available.

Interior of the Silver Platters CD-only store. Shopping in a store like this, with up to 10,000 titles to choose from, can easily whet your appetite for more CDs.

method for financing your conversion to CD. Some stores buy entire collections. If you decide you no longer need your old LP or tape collections, you might try to find such a location. The return you get depends, of course, on the condition of the collection as well as on its contents.

CD PACKAGING AND ACCESSORIES

There are numerous options for storing and maintaining your CD collection. Although a thriving trade is growing up around the CD accessory business, the Compact Disc actually needs little maintenance and comes with a very dependable storage container of its own.

The packaging of an audio recording differs from most other types of packaging in that it is designed to stay with the product. In addition to displaying graphic images relating to the music or performer, the packaging serves as a storage container and provides useful information about the recording. As a result, music packaging has traditionally been a focus of considerable industry attention. And the CD has received its share.

The central element of the CD package is the jewel box, the hinged, plastic case in which the great majority of CDs thus far has been sold. It was patterned after the highly successful cassette case designed earlier by Norelco, a Philips-related company. Both boxes provide a high degree of protection and convenience.

Since packaging also plays an obvious role in influencing your buying decision, it is worth considering some of the variants you may see when you arrive at the CD bins of your favorite outlet. You will be confronted with an assortment of styles, shapes, and sizes designed to catch your attention. The display shelves typically include everything from simple plastic-wrapped jewel boxes to elaborately packaged multidisc collections.

Originally, CDs were simply sold in their shrink-wrapped jewel boxes. This is often still the case with many classical CDs. While such simple packaging was a practical choice, retail stores complained that the small format of the box created certain problems. For one, their display bins were built to accommodate the standard LP cover. Furthermore, its compact size made the jewel box more subject to pilferage. Record-label art departments, as well, expressed concern at the loss of cover space for artwork and contents information.

Such issues forced labels to try better ways of designing and packaging their CDs. The use of standard 12″ × 12″ LP dimensions for a CD package was proposed, but the industry opted instead to create new shelving design to accommodate a narrower format. The simplest approach has been the so-called *blister pack*. This clear, molded 5½″ × 11″ plastic shell allows the manufacturer to display the disc in its jewel box with both covers of the enclosed printed booklet clearly visible. This method has proved economical to produce and requires no additional graphics. What's more, two blister packs, side by side, fit neatly and conveniently into existing LP bins.

A second approach, used primarily for pop and rock CDs, is the cardboard pack. It conforms to the blister-pack dimensions but it conceals the disc and jewel box inside a thin, printed cardboard box, shrink-wrapped in clear plastic. The artwork and contents information are usually reproduced on the package's exterior. Although the cardboard pack is somewhat more costly to the

manufacturer, this is not typically reflected in a higher list price.

Two-disc sets are often sold in a back-to-back double jewel box, which may be shrink-wrapped or in a double-thick blister pack or cardboard package. Larger multidisc sets, such as operas or collections, may sometimes appear in 12″ × 12″ boxes with graphics resembling a standard LP package.

A few attempts have been made to forego the jewel box entirely and package CDs in cardboard sleeves and paper dust jackets resembling miniature LP covers. In general, these experiments have met

Cardboard packaging of CDs. The newer style of CD packaging involves a cardboard pack that can accommodate larger graphics. Most pop and rock CDs now come with the jewel-boxed disc packaged inside these cardboard containers.

with strong opposition from consumers and created a storm of debate within the industry. Most critics predicted that flimsy packaging would undermine the CD's high-quality image. Many consumers complained that it did not provide adequate protection for the disc and created storage problems by not fitting well with jewel-boxed discs.

Despite the controversy, it is quite likely that alternative packaging and display approaches will continue to appear. Such experimentation will likely contribute to price drops in the future as labels agree on the most cost-effective and efficient way to display their goods.

Remember, the appearance of a CD package is important primarily for what it tells you about the disc inside and for the protection and storage it offers. If the jewel box doesn't meet your storage needs, however, you can probably find something that does in the accessories section

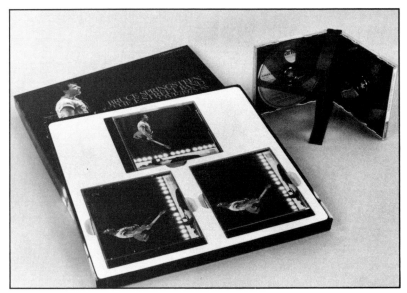

at almost any CD retailer. Most stores offer a wide range of products to support your CD collection.

Disc Containers

A variety of sensible CD accessories is designed for the storage and transportation of your discs. Such systems can be useful at home by helping you maintain order among your discs as your collection grows. In the car or on the run, travel carriers can help

Multidisc packaging. Double CD albums often come packaged in the double jewel box shown at right. For three or more CDs, boxed sets are more practical. Some multidisc operas are packaged simply as a set of shrink-wrapped jewel boxes.

protect them from damage.

If you prefer attractive styling and space-conscious design, any number of home storage systems are available to complement your stereo center. These units are designed to store the CD in its

Alternative CD packaging. The disc on the left is contained in a paper sleeve that fits in a cardboard cover, much like an LP record. The disc at the upper right comes in a 3-panel fold-out, one of which contains a molded plastic holder for the disc. The package at the lower right shows a slip-cover for a jewel box. None of these alternatives to the jewel box has found much acceptance.

jewel box. For instance, you will find units shaped like Rolodex files, Carousel trays, Flip 'N File rotary action modules . . . ; in black plastic, smoked plastic, woodgrain, solid oak, solid teak, hand-oiled, laminated, wall-mountable . . . ; with one drawer, two drawers, rolltops, matched-key locking doors, one-touch securing-release mechanisms, interlocking modules . . . ; providing horizontal storage, vertical storage, linear storage . . . ; on swivel-base, slide-out tray, mar-resistant

Compact Disc storage units. A wide variety of CD storage units—in various styles and materials—is available, usually in CD and record stores.

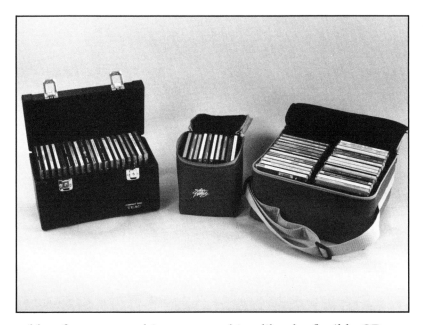

Compact Disc carrying cases. For portable and auto units, CD carrying cases are handy for keeping discs organized.

rubber feet . . . ; and in combination racks for computer floppy/CD, video tape/CD, cassette/CD racks, and so on. The array of available units is quite astounding and continues to grow. Prices can range from $10 for the simpler plastic units to hundreds of dollars for the better-designed, wood-cabinet models.

For traveling in the car or for use at the beach, you might want to choose something like the flexible CD-sized wallet that holds up to 10 discs—in leather or nylon, with velcro fasteners or buttons and snaps. These units are designed to hold only the discs; you can leave the jewel boxes at home. The discs are easily taken in or out, and the disc pouches are lined with soft, nonabrasive material to provide an extra measure of protection. If you want something a little more sturdy with greater disc ca-

pacity, there are briefcase-style carrying cases that hold up to 50 or 60 CDs. Prices in this category can range from $10 to over $100.

Other CD storage accessories include simple replacement jewel boxes, for about a dollar, in case one gets broken. And if you feel like trying something new, you will find alternative jewel boxes such as the three-hinged box popular in Japan. This type has a folding back panel which allows for easier opening and closing of the box.

Most accessories can be found at any CD retail store. However, if you need additional cartridges for multi-disc players as well as single-disc cartridges for auto players, you will probably have to go back to the stereo store where you bought the player.

Disc Cleaners

Just as record cleaners have been the best-selling LP accessory for many years, CD cleaner kits seem likely to follow suit. While dust and dirt buildup on CDs is far less crucial to the performance of the disc, it can nonetheless hinder the player's ability to read the data encoded there. If the plastic underside of a disc gets covered with scrapes and smudges, the laser may not be able to focus properly on the data in the pits. And deep scratches on the top, label side of a disc can render portions of the music unplayable. The cleaner and more protected you can keep your discs, the better and more problem-free their performance will be.

Unlike LPs, which require you to brush or wipe the surface in the direction of the grooves, it is recommended that CDs be cleaned with strokes radiating out from the center. In this way, any scratching that might occur in the course of cleaning will not obscure linear stretches along the spiral of pits. If you take good care of your CDs, storing them in the jewel box, and handling them carefully by the edges, you really should not need a disc cleaner. If a disc gets smudged or soiled it is perfectly acceptable to clean it gently with soap and water or wipe it with a soft cloth. If you are a high-tech enthusiast, however, you will find an entire arsenal of cleaners and cleaning devices to accomplish the same thing.

At its most basic, a cleaning system will consist of a simple spray solution and nonabrasive foam pads for manual cleaning and polishing of the discs. This type of cleaner typically may cost from $5 to $10. More elaborate systems may involve an enclosure into which you place the disc and a motorized turntable for spinning it while the surface is sprayed and wiped with internal buffing pads. These may sell for upwards of $150. If a disc cleaner appeals to you, look primarily for gentle, nontoxic cleaning solutions and nonabrasive cloths and brushes.

Compact Disc cleaners. If you handle your discs roughly, a cleaner might be a good idea. Carefully handled discs should not require any cleaning other than wiping with a soft cloth.

PART FOUR

The CD in Perspective

CHAPTER 9

The CD Story

CD's ROOTS

A system as complex and successful as the Compact Disc did not appear without precursors. The CD success story builds on two trends that have developed over the past century: first, the growing popularity of prerecorded music for home entertainment, begun with Edison's invention of the phonograph in 1876; and second, the rapid advancements in the past 20 years in storing information on laser-read discs and using computer chips to process sound digitally. This combination of an established market and new technologies coalesced in 1982 with the introduction of the CD.

Prerecorded Music

Today's recording industry is based on a fact that became apparent soon after the introduction of the phonograph: consumers around the world will avidly support the creation of ever better devices on which to hear their favorite music reproduced in the privacy of their own homes.

The first Edison phonograph, although primitive when judged by today's standards, created quite a sensation. Early models of the machine were demonstrated to incredulous heads of state, awed by the first system to record and reproduce sound. But Edison made sure that the benefits of the phono-

graph reached the common consumer, too. Within a few years of its invention, the new technology had been successfully introduced all over the world.

A long string of steady improvements followed. In 1887, Emile Berliner introduced the first flat record, or disc. With his record label, American Graphophone, came the birth of the recording industry. After the turn of the century, consumer demand had developed to such an extent that music by well-known performers of the day began to be available for purchase. A major record industry principle was formed: "Talent Sells."

The limited technical demands of the popular music of the 1930s and 1940s made it an ideal art form for the recording medium. Sales finally began to pull the industry upright. What had begun as an amusing parlor device rapidly became an integral part of the adolescent socialization process.

The 1950s and the 1960s saw the process accelerate as stereo records and then recordable cassette tapes found widespread acceptance. Part of the key to this success was the standardization of the formats. All records would play on virtually all turntables, all tapes would play on all cassette decks. During the 1970s, sales of cassettes increased steadily, and by 1983, tapes outsold records. The LP was beginning its decline.

Digital Audio and Optical Discs

As the market for vinyl records and magnetic tape cassettes developed in the years after World War II, the digital audio and laser technologies required for the Compact Disc were gradually evolving in fields other than the recording industry.

In the forties, the first computers appeared. The U.S. Army developed ENIAC (Electronic Numerical Integrator and Computer), a machine that electronically processed digital data to compute ballistic trajectories. The machine weighed 30 tons and contained 18,000 vacuum tubes, which generated an immense amount of heat. Its processing power was still far less than what's packed into today's CD player.

To make computers practical, the tube technology had to go. Its replacement, the transistor, was smaller and generated less heat. This innovation led to the first large business computers used for digital data processing in the fifties and sixties. The next breakthrough was the development of the integrated circuit, or microchip, in the sixties. This device combined the equivalent of hundreds of transistors on a chip no larger than a thumbnail. The seventies and eighties saw dramatic increases in the number of circuits that could be integrated on a single chip, leading to the development of personal computers.

Even before the first computers were built, the basic theory of sampling communications data—such as an audio signal—was proven mathematically by the American engineer Harry Nyquist. His theorem, published in 1928, provides the basis for the CD's 44.1-kHz sampling rate which reproduces sounds up to the 20-kHz limit of human hearing. Further expanding on Nyquist's work, C. E. Shannon published in 1948 the communications theories that led to the practical development of pulse code modulation (PCM), the method of audio encoding used in the Compact Disc.

The same digital advances that were spurring the data processing industry brought changes to the recording studios. By the mid-sixties the first PCM digital audio recorder was created which stored the audio as digital data on video tape. The next decade saw increasing use of digital audio components of many types in professional recording studios. By the late 1970s, some record labels were regularly creating digital masters for LPs. Digital audio technology, by then refined in the professional realm, was ready for introduction to the consumer.

Only one more thing was needed: a convenient, high-density storage medium. The solution appeared in the form of the optical disc, whose data are both encoded and played back by means of low-powered lasers.

The first laser appeared in 1960. In the decade that followed, companies such as MCA, Philips, and Thomson experimented with optical information storage. The first

won the interest of popular artists.

1928—Harry Nyquist publishes sampling theorem that forms the basis of digital audio recording systems.

1931—RCA demonstrates first 33⅓-rpm LP.

1940—*Billboard* magazine introduces record industry charts.

1943—ENIAC, first electronic computer, built at University of Pennsylvania.

1947—First magnetic tape recorders sold in U.S.

1948—John Bardeen, William Shockley, and Walter Brattain invent the transistor at Bell Laboratories.

—C. E. Shannon publishes theories for development of pulse code modulation (PCM). ▶

consumer product using an optical disc was the Laser-Vision videodisc, which stored an hour of *analog* video on each side of the 12-inch-diameter disc. Developed and marketed by MCA, Philips, and Pioneer, the LaserVision videodisc proved that the technical challenges presented by a laser-read disc could be solved for a consumer product, thus proving much of the practical basis for the development of the CD.

THE BIRTH OF THE COMPACT DISC

The technical success of the laser videodisc stimulated research to create an audio format using optical disc storage. The increased data capacity of optical discs meant that audio could be stored and reproduced *digitally*, providing sound quality far superior to LPs and cassettes.

In the late 1970s, as many as nine different prototypes of digital audio optical discs were in development in research labs around the world. But no single company wanted to introduce an audio disc that might prove incompatible with other, subsequent formats. Philips and Sony had learned this lesson from video formats. Philips's LaserVision was hampered by competing videodisc formats from JVC and RCA. Sony's Beta videotape has gradually lost ground to the VHS format. Neither company wanted similar problems in the audio market, which had proved resistant to incompatible standards.

So these two highly competitive giants in the electronics industry had the foresight to agree upon a common set of standards for an optical audio disc. The Philips/Sony alliance, bolstered by the strength of one of the world's largest record companies, Philips-owned PolyGram, was powerful enough to forge a single standard. And by licensing the basic technology, it made most of the world's other hardware and software producers recognize that the CD was a far preferable alternative to a jungle of mismatched formats. In 1981, 35 hardware manufacturers adopted the Philips/Sony standard as the Compact Disc Digital Audio standard, and the race to bring this technology to market began.

Drawing on its experience with developing the LaserVision videodisc, Philips contributed mainly to the precise laser-tracking optical systems of the Compact Disc. Engineers at Sony, already experienced in digital recording systems, perfected the sophisticated digital-encoding and error-correction schemes for storing audio on the disc. Both companies worked out their own techniques and processes for player and disc manufacturing.

The basic laser disc and digital audio technology must be the same in every player and disc bearing the CD logo. This standardization ensures that any disc will play in any player. But the standard was flexible enough to allow for wide variations in the style, features, and audio enhancements of players from different manufacturers. This allowed rival companies to compete while at the same time adhering to a common standard.

Philips and Sony were convinced that the CD product had a great deal of merit. The CD's sound quality, durability, and convenience were clear advantages over the LP. Although the first players—introduced in 1982 in Japan—were priced at over $1000 and the discs at almost $20, those prices were sure to come down as volume increased. A curious record industry watched to see whether this latest in a long series of "gimmicks" for the

by NHK Technical Research Institute.

1971—Intel and other chip makers release first Large Scale Integration (LSI) microchips.

1973—Denon and BBC begin digital recording for use as master tapes for LP releases.

1977—Telarc and a few other small labels begin to produce and promote digitally mastered records.

1978—Philips releases a laser-scanned videodisc player under the Magnavox brand.

1981—Thirty-five electronics manufacturers agree on the Philips/Sony standard for the Compact Disc Digital Audio.

1982—First commercial CD players sold in Japan and Europe. ▶

home entertainment consumer would meet with popular approval. No one knew whether the CD would succeed.

The outcome is now obvious. Much of the CD's success in the U. S. can be attributed to a marketing organization known as "The Compact Disc Group." This amalgamation of hardware manufacturers, record labels, and others was formed in the spring of 1983 to give everyone in the CD business a chance to work together establishing this new product. The CD Group held regular forums where its members openly discussed common problems in reaching a wary consumer with an untried technology.

When the CD Group began, a mere handful of companies were producing hardware. The only players available were home models which carried price tags in excess of $600—in short, toys for audiophiles.

Only a few labels had released discs. Most of these were classical or jazz, the two largest markets for quality recordings. Relatively few rock or pop CDs were in stores, since the primary buyers for that market—people between 15 and 25—were presumed to have less concern for audio quality, and even less money to invest in high-tech laser records. Country and folk music CDs were nowhere to be heard.

Facilities for the production of discs, moreover, were abysmally insufficient. Only two high-volume plants existed—PolyGram's Hannover facility in West Germany and Sony's plant in Japan. Together with a few smaller facilities scattered around the world, they were hardly able to turn out more than a few thousand discs per day. In light of the fact that a single hit album can sell millions of copies in a matter of months, CD production was clearly in its infancy.

The CD Group went to

work solving both the technical and marketing problems faced in launching a new consumer product. The member companies sponsored educational publications and consumer awareness programs; they set standards for disc packaging; and they cooperated in cross-promotional efforts to convince the American public that both players and discs were worth the investment.

CD's first year was a small beginning. In 1983, only 30,000 players and 800,000 discs were sold in the U.S. The following year proved to be a time for addressing problem areas and setting firm foundations for the growth of the new format. Early difficulties with disc tracking and player design were ironed out. More stereo and record stores began to carry CD products. And the appearance of *Digital Audio and Compact Disc Review* magazine—devoted primarily to the CD—helped create a

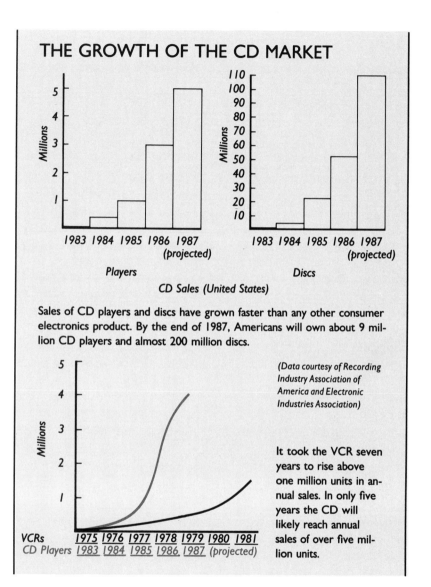

THE GROWTH OF THE CD MARKET

CD Sales (United States)

Players

Discs

Sales of CD players and discs have grown faster than any other consumer electronics product. By the end of 1987, Americans will own about 9 million CD players and almost 200 million discs.

(Data courtesy of Recording Industry Association of America and Electronic Industries Association)

It took the VCR seven years to rise above one million units in annual sales. In only five years the CD will likely reach annual sales of over five million units.

climate for expanding the market.

In 1985, consumer realization of the CD's benefits finally blossomed. Player sales hit the million mark, fueled by a Christmas buying frenzy that left many stereo stores out of CD stock. By this time, all major labels had issued CD products, spurring disc sales to over 22 million. The efforts of the Compact Disc Group were so successful that in November 1985, the group disbanded, its mission to firmly establish CD accomplished.

In 1986, the CD market swelled to sales levels of 3 million players and 53 million discs. The year 1987 began with over 200 CD player models on the market, with projected sales above 4 million for the year. Almost 10,000 different CD titles were available from over 200 labels in the U.S. And as additional pressing plants come on line, the U.S. will likely produce over 100 million audio Compact Discs in 1987.

THE VERSATILE COMPACT DISC

CD-Audio

While the audio Compact Disc has emerged as an astounding success in the consumer electronics market, it is also finding application in other fields. Its sound quality, durability, and random-access capabilities make it ideal as a replacement for many older, traditional media as well as the solution to many long-standing problems involving accurate, dependable, automated music systems.

Perhaps the earliest use of the CD beyond the living room or car was for radio broadcasts. Its ease of use in the control booth and its noticeably improved sound won enthusiastic praise from DJs, engineers, program directors, listeners, and, therefore, ad buyers. In the early days of CD, radio stations were frustrated by the limited supply of discs and the

several-month time lag between an album's release and its appearance on CD. But the market has solved those problems, and radio's support has helped millions become aware of the change taking place in the buying habits of music consumers.

Although off-the-shelf commercial CD players are adequate for radio broadcasts, many stations opt for specialized models. These professional players are more rugged and offer features such as precise positioning of the laser at the beginning of a track and automatic pause at the end of a track. Some FM radio stations have automated CD systems to broadcast uninterrupted programs of music. Multidisc players with high programmability are providing stations with a useful new tool for this purpose.

Of course, automated music systems are not limited to radio stations. The first coin-operated phonograph appeared at the Palais Royal Saloon in San Francisco in 1889. Since that time innovations in recorded music—such as the 45 and stereo—have each spawned their own versions of the *jukebox*. The CD is no different in this respect. In mid-1986, the Seeburg Corporation, a leading manufacturer of jukeboxes in the U.S. since 1907, introduced the *LaserMusic* CD jukebox.

This high-power CD jukebox holds up to 60 discs for a total of some 1000 possible selections (conventional jukeboxes offer only about 200 choices). The player design reflects considerable utilization of CD technology. Whereas most earlier jukeboxes have incorporated less than spectacular hi-fi components, the LaserMusic boasts a 200-watt amplifier and a powerful three-way speaker system. The front panel includes various digital read-

The Seeburg *LaserMusic* CD jukebox, which holds 60 discs and gives you three plays for a dollar.

outs and volume meters as well, lending a further high-tech air to the player.

The price of a play also reflects the new world of CD. The machine accepts either a one-dollar bill for 3 plays, or a five-dollar bill for 18 plays. Remote controls allow bartenders or restaurant managers to control volume and selection from other areas of the establishment.

The durability, size, and dependability of CD systems make them attractive for a wide variety of public music applications. Not only do they take up less room in areas where space is at a premium, but they offer trouble-free maintenance, longer playing time, and for now, a high-tech image boost. Such CD background music systems are beginning to appear in offices and shopping areas.

Another place you will find this new application is in the skies overhead. Commercial airlines have offered their passengers in-flight music over personal headphones for several decades. But the sound has traditionally been of extremely poor quality because of the low frequency range and high signal-to-noise ratio of most current tape-based systems and uncomfortable, low-quality headsets.

But now, a company called TransCom has begun to promote CD-based systems designed specifically for use in airliners. The units can handle either cassette tapes or CDs and are designed to fit right into existing cabin spaces. As new generations of jets are built with the CD in mind, higher-quality headphone connections will offer digital sound to passengers at 30,000 feet.

The CD is also becoming a mainstay in the professional recording studio for the distribution of sound effects and production music. For years, sound engineers have had to search through tapes or use scratchy records to find the right sound effect or background music for an advertising jingle. Now the CD makes it easy to locate the desired sound—and at a higher level of quality.

COMPACT DISC MARKET FACTS

The CD is now firmly established as a viable and enduring product for a number of sound economic reasons:

• **Overwhelming Acceptance by Consumers.** The CD has become the fastest-growing consumer electronic product ever. Analysts estimate that by the end of 1987 more than 13 percent of all U.S. households with a stereo system will also have a CD player. That's a cumulative installed base of about seven million players.

• **Unprecedented Price Reductions.** The first CD player on the U.S.

market retailed for over $1000. Two and a half years later a CD player was offered by a discount dealer for $137. This price drop, almost 90 percent, is reminiscent of the early price wars of the now ubiquitous pocket calculator.

• **Single International Standard.** Every Compact Disc will play on every CD player everywhere in the world. The unfortunate incompatibility obstacles that hampered consumer acceptance of computers (Apple vs. IBM) and VCRs (Beta vs. VHS) are unknown in the CD marketplace. There are no other digital audio disc formats.

• **Established Distribution Channels.** The Compact Disc is sold in every major record outlet in this country. The sales curve is so staggering that a growing percentage of retailers have converted largely (or exclusively) to CD sales. Compact Disc hardware is sold through traditional hi-fi dealers and discount retailers under virtually every major brand name of audio equipment. Even turntable manufacturers are converting to the CD business.

• **Long-term Replacement Product.** Just as LPs replaced 78-rpm records, the CD is certain to replace the LP/turntable combination. With surveys showing turntables in an estimated 75 million U.S. households, the replacement market for CD is immense.

• **Massive Industrial Investment in CD.** Major multinational corporations are committing billions of dollars to supplying the growing demand for Compact Discs. For example, the joint venture Philips and DuPont Optical Company was created to produce CDs and other optical discs, with an expected investment of $500 million by 1990.

• **Audio Is Only the Tip of the CD Iceberg.** The CD is a true digital medium that will eventually find wide applications beyond music playback. It will be used for electronic publishing as well as for interactive audio/visual entertainment and education products. The multimedia capability of the Compact Disc is only now beginning to be explored. The medium's versatility and resultant additional markets will ensure that the economies of scale continue to drive down the price of this technology.

CD-ROM

Although the Compact Disc was originally designed to store audio, it can be used to store any type of digital data. Already this capability is appearing in the computer industry. The CD-ROM (Read-Only-Memory) version of the disc can store a massive amount of data that can be accessed with a computer and displayed on its screen. Since 1985, more than a hundred CD-ROM titles have been made, offering everything from electronic encyclopedias to medical data bases, giving fingertip access to bookshelves' worth of information.

CD-ROM requires the use of a specialized player, called a CD-ROM drive. Functioning as a computer *peripheral* device, it connects to a variety of home and business computers via standard connectors. It is not a stand-alone device that can work on its own since a computer is required to access and display the data on the disc. Some CD-ROM drives can also play audio discs, so that when you're not accessing a data base you can listen to your favorite music.

Rightfully considered the first offspring of the marriage of the CD and the computer, the CD-ROM format is a hybrid tool aimed primarily at the business environment. The CD-ROM disc looks exactly like the Compact Disc you buy in the record stores, but in this format it can store the data from as many as 1500 regular floppy discs. That's over five hundred *megabytes* of data—the equivalent of 500 million characters of text.

Unlike a magnetic floppy disc used with computers, a CD-ROM disc cannot record data the user might want to electronically "write" on the disc (hence the term *Read-Only-Memory*). As a result, its primary application is the distribution of prerecorded information, generally large data bases.

The Amdek LASERDRIVE-1 CD-ROM drive. When connected to a personal computer, this CD-ROM drive serves up megabytes of computer data. And when you're not using it for data base retrieval, the same unit will play your music discs.

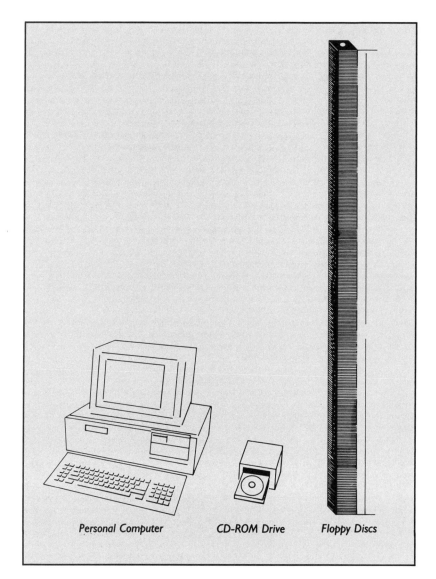

Personal Computer   CD-ROM Drive   Floppy Discs

The first general-purpose CD-ROM product was Grolier's *Electronic Encyclopedia*. The text data from the original bound version of 20 volumes, when digitized and indexed, filled only about 25 percent of the available space on a single disc. The CD-ROM's search and retrieval software lets you manipulate the data on the CD much like you would in book form. You can choose the desired alphabetical volumes from a menu. For instance, if you want to look up Thomas Edison, you first choose the "E" volume. A secondary menu gives you listings of entries in this volume, including one on "Edison, Thomas Alva," which you can then read—page by page—on the screen.

But the real power of the computer/CD-ROM combi-

The incredible storage capacity of a CD-ROM disc is equivalent to the data you could fit on about 1500 floppy discs for an IBM PC.

nation is its ability to search the entire data base electronically in ways that would be impractical in print form. For example, you could search the encyclopedia for all occurrences of the word "Edison" and you would find that it appears 91 times in 41 articles, with titles ranging from "Centennial Exposition" to "World's Fairs." The software then lets you access any of those articles directly, taking you straight to the target word within seconds.

Other CD-ROM application areas include reference data bases for business, education, libraries, hospitals, government—any number of uses where large amounts of information need to be accessed quickly. In mid-1987, the software company Microsoft released a CD-ROM product entitled "Microsoft Bookshelf," which includes such standard desktop references as *The American Heritage Dictionary*, *Roget's Thesaurus*, *The World Almanac*, *The Chicago Manual of Style*, *Bartlett's Familiar Quotations*, the *U.S. Zip Code Directory*, a spelling–checker, various letter and document forms, and a listing of nationwide business information sources. The disc runs on any standard CD-ROM drive and can be used with a number of standard word-processing systems. It offers writers an electronic reference library at their fingertips.

Other data bases include law, business, stock and news indexes, parts catalogs, service manuals, and telephone directories. CD-ROM can even be a life saver in certain cases. The Rocky Mountain Poison Center has released its massive *Poisindex* on CD-ROM disc. This listing of some 370,000 poisons, with their antidotes, is at the heart of emergency rooms across the country. The immense size of the data base makes a printed listing difficult to use in crisis situations. But the CD-ROM version provides fast access, and the software even allows for instant computation of the correct antidote dosage when the body weight of the individual is entered into the computer.

But the CD-ROM is not limited to the storage of text alone. Video, graphics, and audio can be a part of the information stored on the disc and accessed by the user. While graphics are not uncommon to computer programs and games, the addition of high-quality images and full-fidelity audio make CD-ROM a powerful new contender on the computer market.

Foreign language programs, for instance, are ideal for the CD-ROM medium. Not only can extensive multilingual audio be stored on disc, but supportive text and graphics can make the material more interesting. And the interactive nature of the medium allows for sophisticated training and practice sessions.

An example of this technology put to work is the *Facts-On-File Visual Dictionary CD-ROM*, a prototype product created in 1986. The disc—based on the book *The Visual Dictionary*—stores pictures of common objects and their names. Using a computer pointing device called a *mouse*, you select a picture

The Facts on File Visual Dictionary CD-ROM. This prototype disc contains graphic images of hundreds of common items, each with its parts identified and spoken in both French and English.

and then a part of the object. The computer responds with the name of the part on the screen as well as spoken audio of the name of the part. You can choose which language you want to see and hear—English or French. The product operates on both IBM and Apple computers.

Maps can be stored in CD-ROM as well. Detailed road maps, navigational charts, and flight maps are all find-ing their way onto the CD-ROM format. Even the developing field of desktop publishing has been boosted by CD-ROM. With sophisticated text and graphic editing software and high-quality laser printers, the computer industry has made typeset-comparable publishing possible in the average business office. The CD-ROM is being readied for storage of visual images, logos, and designs that will act as an integral part of such a system.

All these computer applications of CD-ROM are realities today. In the CD's short lifespan of only five years it has found numerous uses beyond music entertainment. But this is only the beginning. Visionary leaders in communications technology have many other uses and markets in mind for the versatile Compact Disc.

CHAPTER 10

Future CD Developments

The LP and the cassette tape have served us well for many years as carriers of high-fidelity music. Progress in both technologies has refined the sound quality and improved the audio performance of each. But both formats are destined to remain in the analog audio realm.

Unlike the LP and cassette, the Compact Disc is a versatile and adaptable medium suited for many uses beyond home music playback. The CD-ROM format has already proven that. But there are many more advances in store for the digital discs—increased capabilities that are not mere fantasies but are actual products in various stages of development.

The reasons behind the growing versatility of CD products have most to do with the massive storage capabilities, random access, and accuracy of its digital data. Just as the audio CD has revolutionized the world of recorded sound, other versions of the CD will revolutionize the fields of publishing, education, and home entertainment.

The third CD format to reach the market—CD-Video, or CD-V—provides a way of conveniently distributing digital audio and analog video on the same disc. And CD-Interactive, or CD-I, promises to deliver multimedia programming for entertainment and education.

But first, there are many improvements still waiting in the wings for CD-Audio.

CD-AUDIO

Control and Display

CD-Audio players will continue to offer increasingly advanced and convenient features. As manufacturers seek to distinguish their models from the competition, you'll continue to see new and better ways of controlling the player and displaying information from the disc. Look for these features in future models:

- Increased Ease of Programmability. Through the addition of numbered buttons and extra-function buttons, programming your CD player will be made simpler. Separate repeat and auto-pause buttons will likely appear on lower-priced players. In addition, look for more players to store your programmed selections in memory that isn't erased when the power is turned off.

• Improved Time and Graphic Displays. It will be easy for manufacturers to add additional time displays to show simultaneously the elapsed and remaining time of a track, a programmed sequence, or the entire disc. Further, it's likely that you'll see some interesting graphical displays on the front of CD players. Some may represent the playback progress of the disc graphically, while others may show changing-color displays that are generated by the music signal itself.

• Direct Cueing. A few players already allow you to go directly to a specific point on a disc by entering the track number and time point (minutes and seconds) within the track. Look for this on more and more players, along with frame-accurate cueing that allows you to start a track to within $\frac{1}{75}$th-of-a-second accuracy.

• Error Indicators. The error-correction mechanisms in a CD player operate usually without your knowledge—unless they reach a badly damaged part of a disc and mute the sound long enough for you to perceive it, or worse, audibly mistrack. It's entirely possible to have indicator lights on the front panel that light up when errors are encountered and corrected. This feedback could help you evaluate the digital integrity of each disc, giving you (and disc reviewers) additional information about the manufactured quality of the audio on a disc. This feature could become more useful as new disc-

manufacturing techniques introduce more variability in disc quality.

• Display on Remote Control. It's hard to read the track and time information on a player's front panel if you're sitting across the room with your remote control. Soon some players will offer a digital display of that information on the remote control unit itself, without wires connecting the remote to the player.

• Display of Album and Song Titles. Since the CD is a digital medium, it's very feasible to store text along with the audio on a disc. The song titles and album information (title, performer, composers, even lyrics) could then be available for display on new CD players designed for that purpose. Seeing the song title on the player—instead of just a track number—would add another dimension of convenience that would further distinguish the CD from its analog predecessors.

Digital Output

At some point, the digital audio data from the disc must be converted to an analog stereo signal that is then fed to an amplifier or headphone jack. While most CD players do this internally, a few high-end models have digital outputs that connect to a separate unit that does the digital-to-analog conversion.

In the future, more players will offer digital output as an option for connection to a separate converter unit as well as to other digital components that may appear. These could include: digital amplifiers that would help eliminate distortion; digital surround-sound processors to increase spatial realism; and digital equalizers to let you customize the frequency response for your listening room. These units would provide unparalleled control of the sound output from your CD player. Although

amplifiers, surround-sound units, and equalizers are available today in analog form, keeping the audio signal in the digital domain for as many of these steps as possible will help maintain the fidelity and clarity of the sound.

Hardware and Software Configurations

One trend in CD players that seems certain to continue is the multidisc capability. In addition to the cartridge, rack, and platter systems available today, designs with faster access and increased disc storage will provide the ability to keep your entire CD collection at fingertip access. This is another area where increased programmability features will make significant advances.

You can also look for portables to get smaller and lighter, with more features such as programmability and built-in radios. Advances in

battery technology and power consumption efficiencies could make portables much lighter, with longer playing times as well.

Miniaturization will not be limited to the hardware. A new "CD-Single" format is also beginning to appear. The smaller disc—designed to be approximately 3 inches (80 mm) in diameter—holds about 20 minutes of audio. Newly built CD players will have an inset in the disc drawer to accommodate the smaller CDs, while you'll need a simple adapter to play a CD-Single in an existing unit. The CD-Single will provide a cost-effective way to distribute hit singles to radio stations as well as replace 45-rpm records in the consumer marketplace.

Recordability

Perhaps the most oft-asked question about CD is: When can I record on one? The answer is that today you can't. But with rapid advances in technology, that situation may change. Already, computer systems are making use of *write-once* optical discs, where you can record information directly but you can't erase it or record over it.

This technology may soon be applied to the audio CD, but it's likely to be expensive. The recorder itself—which is more complex than a CD player—may well cost thousands of dollars. And the blank discs would probably cost as much as prerecorded CDs. Unless there are significant breakthroughs in cost, the recordable CD will probably find application only in professional and commercial situations. Besides, recordable *digital audio tape* (DAT) will make its presence felt in the market very soon.

NEW CD FORMATS

CD-Video

Hardware and software for the third Compact Disc format, CD-Video (CD-V),

were formally announced in early 1987. The CD-V players and the CD-V discs that reach the market in late 1987 will deliver high-quality audio and video programming as a further extension of the CD format.

The CD-V discs, which will have a gold rather than a silver tint, contain two separate types of information. The inner portion of the disc holds up to 20 minutes of

normal CD digital audio, enough for about four or five hit songs from an album. The outer portion of the disc contains up to 5 minutes of *analog* video (with a digital sound track) stored in the LaserVision format. The new

CD-Video player and discs. This type of player can play audio CDs and videodiscs as well as the new 5-inch CD-Video discs that contain 20 minutes of digital audio and 5 minutes of video.

CD-V players spin the disc faster than a normal CD when playing the video in order to decode the signal.

All CD-V players will play regular CD-Audio discs in addition to the new CD-V discs. And the inner audio-only tracks of CD-V discs will play in regular CD-Audio players. The players will come in two types. First are the portable and home units designed to play only CD-sized discs, either CD-Audio or CD-Video. The portable units may even have their own small TV screen. Then there will be the larger home CD-V units that will accept the CD-sized discs as well as the 8-inch and 12-inch video-discs which are now included in the CD-Video family of products.

CD-Interactive

The fourth Compact Disc format, CD-Interactive (CD-I), is slated for intro-duction by the end of 1988. This new home electronics appliance, which combines audio/video playback with computer capabilities, will provide the foundation for totally new home entertain-ment and information prod-ucts. It may well play a piv-otal role in linking all the components of your home entertainment center.

CD-I is a logical evolution of CD-Audio and CD-ROM. This multimedia, in-teractive CD system is the fourth in a series of world-wide standards for the Com-pact Disc created by Philips and Sony.

To understand CD-I hard-ware, imagine that you have walked into a stereo store shortly after CD-I has ar-rived. When you ask the sales-person to see a CD player, you are given three choices: one that plays audio only, one that plays audio and · video, or one that also con-nects to your TV and with which you can interact using a keyboard or remote con-trol. This third type of player, the CD-I player, is predicted to cost perhaps

DIGITAL AUDIO TAPE

The continued growth of the digital audio market is by no means limited to the optical disc format. Another digital product stirring up consumer in-terest and industry con-troversy is the *digital au-dio tape* (DAT) format. This impending product has met with a certain amount of resistance from the recording industry since it was first proposed in 1986. Industry officials, still leery of too many for-mats, were concerned that the fledgling CD mar-ket might be squelched by the introduction of an-other digital format. Fur-thermore, long-standing industry concerns about home-taping and piracy of music were aroused at the thought of a consumer product that would allow for digital-quality copies. ▶

Yet, despite the industry's hesitancy, DAT has caught the attention of the same consumers who responded so readily to the CD. Indeed, it would seem very likely that the CD/DAT combination is the logical successor to the LP/cassette.

This is not surprising since the DAT format offers distinct advantages over the analog cassette. First, the sound is stored digitally on a cassette roughly ⅔ the size of a standard analog cassette. Rather than the fixed head used in analog tape decks, the DAT player utilizes a rotary head much like the one in a video recorder. The ro-

tary head allows for a much faster scan rate of the data on the tape without requiring a faster tape speed. This means you can fast-forward from one end of the tape to the other in about half a minute or less.

The tape is recordable in various modes, much like current video tape standards which allow for varying—2-hour up to 6-

hour—recording times, with corresponding levels of fidelity.

$500 more than the audio player. And if you can't make up your mind, most audio CD players will also have a connector that will allow you to upgrade the player later to full CD-I capability.

The CD-I capabilities fall into four main categories, all of which can work together

Magnetic tape cassette formats. The analog audio cassette and the DAT cassette (foreground) are specifically designed for the storage of audio. The videotape formats (VHS, Beta, and 8mm) can store between 2 and 6 hours of digital audio when used in conjunction with a PCM processor.

VHS

Audio Cassette

DAT

Beta

8mm

on the same disc. The first one is audio. CD-I plays not only regular CD audio; it provides three additional levels of sound, each corresponding in quality to LP, FM, and AM sound fidelity. Each of these three levels will store sound in either stereo or mono. As you move to lower levels of fidelity, the playing time is increased. In the AM level, you can record over 19 hours of mono audio on a single disc.

Next comes video. The first versions of CD-I will have partial-screen motion video as well as impressive still-frame picture capabilities. The still-frame pictures will look as good as the best studio-quality TV images. Three different types of pictures can be stored on CD-I: still-frame video pictures, quality computer graphics, and cartoon-like animation. Two levels of resolution will be offered: one for today's TV monitors and a second level for high-resolution digital TVs of the future. One

CD-I disc will hold over five thousand video stills.

Third is data storage. Here the full range of over five hundred megabytes of text will be available just like a CD-ROM disc. And the text can be displayed at either low resolution (40 characters each on 20 lines) or high resolution (80 characters each on 40 lines).

Finally, there is software—software not only to control the program interaction but also for graphics animation, data base retrieval, and synchronized audio/visual output. And because every CD-I disc must play on every CD-I player, each player must have the same set of chips. These include one megabyte of memory and a Motorola 68000 series CPU (as used in the Apple Macintosh, Commodore Amiga, and Atari 520ST computers) as well as proprietary audio- and video-processing chips developed specifically for CD-I.

If this sounds like a CD player with a computer built

into it, that's because it is. Of course, there's no built-in floppy disc drive (at least initially), so you can't input and store your own data. It's intended as a read-only device, with very rich audio and visual output controlled by the user.

CD-I players won't be sold like personal computers, either. Instead, you'll buy them in your stereo store alongside other audio and video equipment. Nor will they work very much like personal computers. You'll hook the CD-I machine up to your TV, and you'll control it with a pointing device or remote control (or even a keyboard on some models). But the experience of using CD-I will be much different from using a computer. You'll get a wide range of rich audio and visual output unlike the beeping sound and poor-quality graphics of a desktop computer.

Again the important consumer advantage is that all CD-I discs will play on all

CD-I machines. You will not be faced with the Apple vs. IBM vs. Commodore incompatibility problems that have stifled the growth of the home computer market. CD-I will be a true home entertainment product: no "boot errors," no "disc formatting." Just insert the disc and push START.

The discs will include a wide range of types of programs, such as an interactive *Sesame Street* for preschoolers, an audio/visual adventure game, an interactive tour of London where you choose which streets you want to explore, a do-it-yourself car repair program, or a talking book.

It could make feasible a multimedia encyclopedia with pictures and sound. Imagine that when you look up an entry for John F. Kennedy, you get not only the text of an article but video-quality pictures from his life as well as audio excerpts of his speeches. The richness of information available to us will expand in quantum leaps with the advent of multimedia interactive discs.

THE ELECTRONIC HOME OF THE TWENTY-FIRST CENTURY

With such impressive developments in electronics technology as this decade has already produced, one can well imagine what the properly equipped home of the coming century may look like. The computer will have long since proven its ability to manage numerous household functions, and as its technology continues to become integrated with audio/video equipment, the "smart" home entertainment center will emerge. Some of the possible innovations to look for by the year 2010 include:

• **Voice-activated Controls.** Advances in voice-recognition hardware and natural-language-interpretation software are paving the way for practical, economical voice control of appliances. Some preliminary products—with limited capabilities—are already on the market. You might not even need a remote for your CD player. Just tell it: "Play track seven."

• **Integrated Household Data Network.** The home of the year 2010 will have wires connecting all appliances, audio/video units, computers, and telephones in a complete home control system. Computers will manage the cooking, lighting, heating, and security systems, and will provide many conveniences for entertainment and education. The Compact Disc will play a key role in providing audio, video, and control data for these systems.

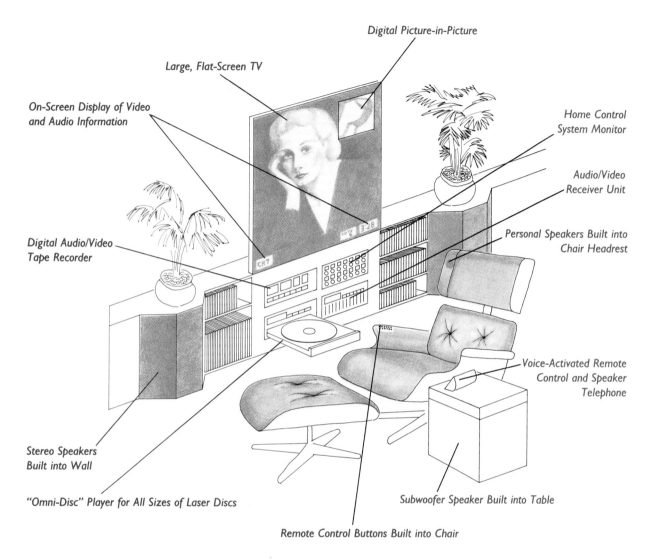

Digital Picture-in-Picture

Large, Flat-Screen TV

On-Screen Display of Video and Audio Information

Home Control System Monitor

Audio/Video Receiver Unit

Digital Audio/Video Tape Recorder

Personal Speakers Built into Chair Headrest

Voice-Activated Remote Control and Speaker Telephone

Stereo Speakers Built into Wall

"Omni-Disc" Player for All Sizes of Laser Discs

Subwoofer Speaker Built into Table

Remote Control Buttons Built into Chair

The home entertainment center of the twenty-first century. Sight and sound will create more realism and convenience for the consumer of the future.

• **Complete Digital Data Systems.** The digital versions of audio disc, audio tape, and computer are already here. In two decades, TVs, VCRs, other audio components, and telephones will make the leap to the digital domain, all offering enhanced capabilities.

• **New Audio/Visual Output Devices.** The flat-screen TV is already on its way to your living room—and any other place in the house where you might find it hard to fit a conventional TV. Wireless audio speakers, perhaps digitally tuned to the CD's output, will be integrated into the walls and furniture of the house.

• **Increased Miniaturization.** Electronic components are getting smaller and faster all the time. Advances in battery technology will reduce weight for portable units. New integrated power circuits will become smaller and cheaper. And advances in optical storage and data compression will cram more and more information onto smaller and smaller discs or tapes (or cards).

• **More Powerful Home Recording Equipment.** The video camera craze is only the start. Next will come easier and cheaper audio and video recording and editing equipment, all of which will be integrated with electronic photography and color laser printers.

• **Increased Distribution of Information.** As the Compact Disc revolutionizes and integrates electronic publishing, more information will also be distributed to homes via satellite and cable networks. The information age is truly upon us.

ELECTRONIC GLOBAL PUBLISHING

The audio Compact Disc is a success because it provides real benefits to buyers in an existing market. As the shining star of consumer electronics in the 1980s, the CD has spawned a giant industry for the manufacture of both the players and the discs. This standard will carry the thrust of recorded music well into the twenty-first century.

What also seems certain is that the Compact Disc will go far beyond music and into the realms of broad-based distribution of information. The various worldwide CD standard formats—CD-Audio, CD-ROM, CD-Video, and CD-Interactive—all build on the basic technology of a Compact Disc and a player. What varies is the data stored on the disc and the circuits in the player to process those data. The strength of the CD-Audio market will provide the "jump-start" for the other CD formats, all of which are leading us into a new age of electronic global publishing.

Electronic

The common element of all the CD formats is that they store and process data in *electronic* form—audio, graphics, text, data, software, and video. The CD can accommodate them all.

Equally important, all of them (except motion video, currently) are stored *digitally* on a CD. This allows for manipulation of the data by the processors in the player, giving us more and better combinations of information than could ever be possible with analog systems. And video, too, is headed for the digital domain. The first signs are the current digital TVs and VCRs that store still-frames. Within the next decade, advances in data compression techniques and optical storage densities will give us digital full-motion video on a Compact Disc.

Global

The global aspect of Compact Disc publishing is evidenced by the worldwide scope of the CD standards. CD-Audio hardware and software are totally compatible, as will be the case with CD-Interactive. With these two formats, any disc will play on any player, anywhere in the world. (Because of the variation in TV standards on different continents, the TV format of a CD-Video disc will have to match the video standard of the playback equipment.) What's more, CD-Audio discs will play on all types of players.

CD-I, however, is especially designed for international use. Its video output is compatible with all three major TV standards in the world today. The text and spoken-word portions of a CD-I program can be stored in several languages on the same disc, with the user selecting the desired language.

Publishing

A number of economic factors give the Compact Disc a clear advantage as a mass-publishing medium. All CD formats, including future ones, can be pressed at any CD plant, anywhere in the world. The same basic optical mechanisms and decoding electronics are used in each type of player. And all the components of CD players, especially CD-I's computer hardware, are amenable to integration, miniaturization, and mass production. These economies of scale, driven by the mass-market success of CD audio, will continue to make it easier for more people around the world to join the CD revolution.

So when you drop your favorite music CD into your player and sit back to enjoy it, you might just ponder the implications of that small, silvery disc. Beyond the clear digital sound, a giant step in information distribution is already under way.

Glossary

AAD The SPARS code for analog recording and mixing, with digital mastering.

A–B repeat A CD-player feature that lets you repeat any portion of the disc, from point A to point B, as you specify. Also called loop repeat.

Access time The time it takes the laser pickup to move from one point on a disc to another. Maximum access time is measured for movement from one extreme of the disc to the other.

ADD The SPARS code for analog recording, with digital mixing and mastering.

Amplitude A measurement of the strength of an analog audio signal at a point in time. The higher the amplitude, the louder the sound. Graphically, the amplitude is the height of the waveform.

Analog In audio terms, referring to sound in the form of a continuous electrical signal that is a direct representation of the sound waveform.

Analog-to-digital converter (ADC) An electronic circuit that converts a continuous analog waveform into discrete digital data representing the waveform.

Anti-aliasing filter An electronic circuit that removes extraneous, high-frequency tones from an input signal. If not removed, these tones would interact with lower frequencies to create false audio tones called alias signals.

Audible scanning A CD-player feature that lets you hear the portions of a track when scanning in fast forward or reverse.

Audiophile A consumer with an avid interest in high-quality sound systems and recordings.

Auto-pause A selectable feature on some CD players that automatically puts the player in pause mode at the end of a track.

Auto Scan A selectable CD-player feature that plays the first 10 or 15 seconds of sound from each track as it scans through a disc.

Auto Space   An option found on some CD players which causes the player to pause for three to four seconds between tracks. Specifically designed for CD-to-cassette taping. Also called Auto Silence.

A-weighting   An adjustment to an audio measurement (usually S/N ratio) that compensates for the range of distortion most noticeable to the human ear.

Bit   Short for binary digit. A bit has a value of either 0 or 1 in the binary number system.

Blister pack   The clear, molded 5½″ × 11″ plastic shell packaging that displays the disc in its jewel box with both covers of the enclosed printed booklet clearly visible.

Boom box   A large, portable stereo system that typically includes a cassette-tape player, radio, detachable speakers, and, increasingly, a CD player.

CD-Interactive (CD-I)   The designation given to a multimedia, interactive format of the CD licensed by Philips and Sony.

CD-ROM   Compact Disc Read-Only-Memory, the generic name given the computer data storage format of the CD.

CD-Video (CD-V)   The designation given to 5-inch, 8-inch, and 12-inch optical discs that hold analog video and digital audio.

Changer   A CD player that holds two or more discs and can automatically change play from one disc to another.

Channel   One of the two stereo sound signals, designated left and right.

Channel separation   A measure (in decibels) of the degree to which the sounds from the left and right channels are isolated from one another.

Check codes   Extra data codes added to the digital audio data stream during the error-protection stage of encoding. These codes are later used to restore missing data or to correct erroneous data.

Clean room   An equipment room in a CD plant that is maintained virtually dust-free to reduce particle contamination of discs during the mastering and replication stages of CD manufacturing.

Combi-player   A player that combines CD audio playback with videodisc playback or some other capability.

Compact Disc Digital Audio   The official designation of the CD audio standard licensed by Philips and Sony.

Compression   A recording technique that squelches loud signal peaks and boosts soft passages in order to fit the full range of a recording into a narrower dynamic range. It's done so that softer sections can be played loudly enough to mask the background noise of the system, without the louder passages becoming unpleasantly loud.

Controller   A microprocessor in the control and display system of a CD player that coordinates its overall operation.

Cross Interleaved Reed–Solomon Code (CIRC)   The error-correction coding scheme used in CDs.

Crosstalk   Audible interference between the left and right stereo channels.

DAD   The SPARS code for digital recording, analog mixing, and digital mastering.

DDD   The SPARS code for digital recording, mixing, and mastering.

Decibel (dB)   A unit of measure of the relative difference in strength of two signals. A decibel is one-tenth of a Bel, named after American inventor Alexander Graham Bell (1847–1922).

Decimal equivalent   The decimal number equal in value to a binary number.

De-interleaving   The process of rearranging interleaved data segments into their original order.

Demodulation   The process of changing the modulated signal from the disc back into the digital audio data stream.

Demultiplexing   The process of separating a multiplexed signal, such as the left and right stereo channels of an audio signal, into its original components.

Digital   Represented by digits as discrete numerical information. By contrast, analog means that something is represented as a physical analog.

Digital audio   The representation of sound as numerical data for both recording and playback purposes.

Digital audio tape (DAT)   A consumer electronics product that records and plays back digital audio on small cassettes.

Digital filtering   Output filters that remove unwanted high frequencies before the signal is converted to analog audio. Invariably used in conjunction with oversampling DACs.

Digital output   A connector on a CD player that outputs audio as digital data.

Digital-ready or **digital-compatible**   A dubious advertising claim when applied to any component, such as a speaker or headphone, that does not receive a digital audio signal from a CD player. (Most of these components receive the *analog* output from a CD player.) In some cases, though, components may have digital inputs or outputs specifically designed to handle a digital audio signal from a CD player.

Digital recording   A recording in which the sound was originally captured in digital form.

Digital-to-analog converter (DAC)   An electronic device that converts discrete digital data into a continuous analog signal.

Digitizing   The process of digitally sampling sound. *See* **Sampling**.

Distortion   The harsh fuzziness of tone often heard when system volume is boosted to its upper limits.

Dynamic headroom   A measure of the peak power of an amplifier, which determines its capability to deliver split-second bursts of sound without distortion.

Dynamic range   The difference, in decibels, between the quietest and the loudest recorded signal level a player or disc can produce.

Eight-to-fourteen modulation (EFM)   The process of converting eight-bit values to fourteen-bit values so that the digital data stream can be stored efficiently in the form of pits on a CD.

Electronic global publishing (EGP)   A sweeping term that encompasses all of the information distribution possibilities of the CD.

Equalization (often abbreviated EQ)   A recording technique in which the frequency spectrum of a particular voice or instrument is adjusted.

Error-correction coding (ECC)   The process of using extra data bits to detect the presence of erroneously stored data and to return them to their correct value.

Error protection   The process of expanding and rearranging data to protect against possible errors in the storage medium.

Filtering   The electronic removal of a range of frequencies from a signal. *See* **Anti-aliasing filter**.

Focus   The ability of a CD player to maintain the proper distance between the laser pickup and the spiral track of pits as a disc rotates.

Frame   The smallest accessible unit of audio on a CD. One frame contains $\frac{1}{75}$th of a second of stereo sound.

Frame-accurate cueing   A CD-player option that allows extremely precise cueing of the disc—typically incorporating a dial to enable positioning of the laser pickup to an accuracy of $\frac{1}{75}$th of a second.

Frequency   The rate of vibration or oscillation of a signal, usually measured in hertz or kilohertz. The higher the frequency of a sound, the higher its pitch.

Frequency response   A measure of how accurately and consistently an audio component reproduces the full range of audible frequencies.

Hardware   CD players and other electronic components. Derives from the computer term *hardware*, which refers to computer equipment.

Harmonic   A higher tone produced simultaneously with a fundamental tone, the frequency of the harmonic being an integer multiple of a fundamental frequency.

Hertz (Hz)   A unit of measurement of frequency equal to one vibration per second, named after German physicist, Heinrich R. Hertz (1857–1894). *See also* **Kilohertz**.

Imaging   The sense of spatial relationship within reproduced stereo sound.

Impedance   A measure of resistance to the passage of alternating current given to speakers and headphones. Measured in ohms (Ω).

Index point   An optional subdivision of a track on a CD, often used in long classical pieces to mark successive movements or passages that aren't long enough to merit separate tracks.

Injection molding   The process of injecting molten plastic (polycarbonate) into a mold to form the substrate of a CD.

Interleaving   The process of subdividing the digital audio data stream into segments that are then reordered so that segments originally adjacent to one another will be spread out, or interleaved, on the disc.

Intermodulation (IM) distortion   A type of distortion added by the electronic circuits in an audio component. IM distortion occurs when multiple tones in the recorded signal interact to form unwanted tones, these unwanted tones having frequencies equal to the sum or difference of the frequencies in the original tones.

Interpolation   The process of filling in missing data between adjacent audio samples by calculating their average value.

Jewel box   The plastic (polystyrene) hinged box in which most CDs are packaged.

Karaoke   A form of sing-along entertainment popular in Japan. Karaoke nightclubs use the CD subcode to display lyrics from the disc on TV monitors.

Kilohertz (kHz)   A unit of measurement of frequency equal to 1000 vibrations per second. *See also* **Hertz**.

Land   The flat place between the pits on the spiral track of a CD.

Laser pickup   The mechanism in a CD player that holds the laser and positions it at various points along the disc diameter.

LaserVision   The former tradename for the laser-read videodisc system popularized by Philips, MCA, and Pioneer. In the U.S., LaserVision discs in 5-inch, 8-inch, and 12-inch sizes now come under the CD-Video moniker.

Master disc   A glass disc on which the data for a CD are recorded in preparation for manufacturing.

Mastering   The step in the recording process in which the final stereo mix is converted to the proper format for manufacturing.

Megabyte   A data-storage measurement equivalent to approximately one million characters of text.

Memory   Circuits in a CD player that store a programmed sequence of tracks.

Micrometer   A unit of length equal to one-millionth of a meter (about $\frac{1}{25,000}$ of an inch).

Mixing   The step in the recording process in which the sound from multiple tracks is combined into a two-channel stereo signal.

Modulation   A means of encoding information for storage or transmission. Examples are *pulse code modulation* (PCM) used for storing audio on a CD, and *amplitude modulation* (AM) and *frequency modulation* (FM) used for radio broadcasts.

Monophonic   Recorded and reproduced in a single audio channel. Often shortened to "mono." *See also* **Stereophonic.**

Multiplexing   The process of weaving multiple data streams, such as the left and right channels of a stereo audio signal, into a single, continuous stream of data.

Multitrack recorder   An audio recorder that records on four or more parallel audio tracks.

Muting   The act of silencing the audio output for a fraction of a second when a CD player encounters data errors that it cannot correct or interpolate.

Numeric keypad   A cluster of at least 10 buttons that includes all the digits from 0 to 9, most often used for entering track numbers.

Optical discs   A high-density storage medium whose data are both encoded and played back using low-powered lasers.

Oversampling   A technique in the digital-to-analog conversion process that reads the digital data at two or four times its normal sampling rate of 44.1 kHz. Oversampling is done so that digital filters may be used to remove unwanted upper-frequency signals from the digital audio.

Parity bits   Extra data bits added to the digital audio stream during the error-protection stage of encoding. These bits are later used to correct missing or erroneous data.

Performance   The degree to which a CD player operates properly in such areas as tracking, error correction, and audio reproduction. Also, performance refers to the particular rendition of a piece of music by a musician or singer.

Photodetector   A light-sensitive electrical device that senses the pulses of laser light reflected from the disc and creates an electrical signal that corresponds to the pulses.

Photoresist   A material coating on the surface of a master disc into which a laser burns the pits during the mastering process.

Pits   Microscopic indentations in the plastic substrate of a CD that represent the digital data recorded there. The pits on a CD are about 0.11 micrometers deep and 0.5 micrometers wide, and their length varies from 0.8 to 3 micrometers.

Polycarbonate   The plastic material from which CDs are molded.

Premastering   A step in the CD recording process in which the finished recording is converted into the proper digital format for storage on a CD.

Programmability   A CD-player feature that allows the user to select the order of playback of tracks.

Pulse code modulation (PCM)   The representation of continuous analog signals as discrete pulses of digital data.

Quantization   The scheme of representing amplitude measurements as discrete subdivisions or quanta.

Remastering   The process of taking original recordings and creating new masters, typically for CD reproduction, to upgrade the sound quality.

Remote control   A hand-held device for controlling a CD player from a distance. Most remote controls are wireless, operating on infrared signals.

Sample   The actual measured value of the amplitude of a waveform at a point in time.

Sample-and-hold circuit   An electronic circuit that briefly holds, or stores in memory, the digital value of a sample so that the sample can be further processed for conversion to digital or analog.

Sampler   A CD containing collections of music by various artists, usually from one label.

Sampling   The process of measuring the amplitude of an audio waveform at regular time intervals.

Sampling rate   The rate at which samples are taken. The sampling rate for CD-Audio is 44.1 kHz, or 44,100 times per second (every 22.6 microseconds).

Sensitivity   A measure of loudness that a speaker or headphone delivers for a given amount of amplifier power. Speakers are rated in dB/watt; headphones in dB/milliwatt.

Servomechanisms   Electrical devices that

make small mechanical movements in response to electrical input signals. "Servos" are used to keep the laser on track and in focus.

Signal-to-noise (S/N) ratio   A measure of the difference in level (in decibels) between the system noise within an audio component and the loudest signal it can produce without noticeable distortion.

Software   CDs, as well as LPs and cassettes, that play on audio hardware. Derives from the computer term *software*, which refers to the programs that run on computer hardware.

SPARS code   A three-letter code originated by SPARS (the Society of Professional Audio Recording Studios) that uses the letters *A* or *D* to indicate which of the three steps—recording, mixing, and mastering—were analog or digital. For CDs, the mastering stage is always digital.

Stereophonic   Recorded and reproduced in two audio channels, designated as left and right. Usually shortened to "stereo." *See also* **Monophonic.**

Subcode   Information stored on a CD that includes track and timing information. Additional subcode storage space is available for other data such as text and graphics.

Substrate   The molded plastic portion of a CD.

Switched   Description of an AC power outlet built into a component that supplies power only when the component itself is switched on.

System noise   Audible hiss and hum produced by an audio component when no audio signal is being input to the component.

Technical specifications   Measurements of various aspects of CD-player audio output such as frequency response and signal-to-noise ratio.

Test disc   A CD that may include sound effects, music, and reference tones for testing the audio performance of a CD player.

Three-beam pickup   A laser pickup mechanism that splits the laser beam, creating two secondary beams on either side of the primary beam. The secondary beams are used for tracking control; the primary beam is used for focus and data decoding.

Total harmonic distortion (THD)   A measure of the inherent system noise in a CD system.

Track   A continuous audio segment on a CD identified by a track number. A CD may have as many as 99 tracks. Also, *track* may refer to the continuous spiral track of pits on a CD. Further, in recording jargon, *track* refers to one of several parallel audio channels on a recording system, such as on a 2-track or multitrack recorder.

Tracking   The ability of a CD player's laser beam to properly follow the spiral track of pits as the disc rotates.

Track selection buttons   Buttons on a CD player used for skipping forward or backward among tracks, or going directly to a specified track.

Two-track   An audio recorder that records on two parallel stereo channels.

Unswitched   Description of an AC power outlet built into a component that supplies power whether or not the component itself is switched on.

Videodisc   A disc for the storage and playback of full-motion video.

Watt (W)   A unit of power used to measure the audio capacity of amplifiers, speakers, and headphones, named after Scottish engineer, James Watt (1736–1819).

Waveform   A graphical representation of an audio signal over time that shows such characteristics as frequency and amplitude.

Suggestions for Further Reading and Listening

The New Sound of Stereo, by Ivan Berger and Hans Fantel, New York: New American Library, 1986. Subtitled "The Complete Guide to Buying and Using the Latest Hi-Fi Equipment," this handy book gives lots of up-to-date information about all types of stereo gear.

CD ROM: The New Papyrus, edited by Steve Lambert and Suzanne Ropiequet, Bellevue, Washington: Microsoft Press, 1986. Subtitled "The Current and Future State of the Art," this 600-page collection of overview articles includes some very good ideas on this emerging technology.

Principles of Digital Audio, by Ken C. Pohlmann, Indianapolis: Howard W. Sams & Co., 1985. This thorough yet readable treatise delves into additional detail on most aspects of digital audio, including specifications for the Compact Disc.

Critical Listening (1982) and *Auditory Perception* (1986), audio training courses by F. Alton Everest, available from Mix Publications Inc., Berkeley. These courses, which both use cassette tapes and an accompanying written manual, cover the basics of sound and how we hear it with cogent explanations and many aural examples.

Illustration Credits

P. 5—Paul Ackerman; p. 7—Sansui Electronics Corporation; p. 8—Paul Ackerman; p. 9 top and bottom—Sony Corporation of America; pp. 9 middle, 10—Paul Ackerman; p. 15—Used with permission of Philips International B.V.; pp. 17, 18, 19, 21, 24, 25, 32—Paul Ackerman; p. 34—Sony Corporation of America; pp. 37, 39, 46—Paul Ackerman; p. 48—*Digital Audio and Compact Disc Review*; p. 53—Sansui Electronics Corporation; pp. 54, 55—Sony Corporation of America; p. 56—Courtesy of N.A.P. Consumer Electronics Corporation; p. 57—TEAC Corporation of America; p. 58—Pioneer Electronics (USA) Inc.; p. 59—Panasonic Company; p. 61 top—Sony Corporation of America; p. 61 bottom—Courtesy of N.A.P. Consumer Electronics Corporation; p. 64—Sony Corporation of America; p. 65 top—Recoton Corporation; p. 65 bottom—Hartzell Manufacturing, Inc.; p. 67 left top and bottom—Paul Ackerman; p. 67 right—Sansui Electronics Corporation; pp. 78, 79—Paul Ackerman; p. 89—Alvin Jennings, LaserVideo, Inc.; pp. 90, 91, 93, 98—Paul Ackerman; pp. 99, 100, 101 top—LaserVideo, Inc.; p. 101 bottom—Sony Corporation of America; p. 102 top—LaserDisc Corporation of America; p. 102 bottom—Pioneer Electronics (USA) Inc.; p. 105—Paul Ackerman; p. 108 top—New England Digital Corporation; p. 108 bottom—Fairlight Instruments; pp. 110, 111, 113—Sony Corporation of America; pp. 117, 118, 121, 126, 134, 136, 137, 138, 139, 140, 149—Paul Ackerman; p. 151—Seeburg Corporation; p. 154—Amdek Corporation, 1901 Zanker Road, San Jose, CA 95112; p. 155—Paul Ackerman; p. 156—Grolier Electronic Publishing, Inc.; p. 157—Editions Québec/Amérique, Facts on File, Inc.; p. 162—Courtesy of N.A.P. Consumer Electronics Corporation; p. 164—*Digital Audio and Compact Disc Review*; p. 167—Paul Ackerman.